DELUSIONS
OF
GRANDEUR

JASON NAJUM

You don't know me. I am not famous. There is no particular reason for you to read this or care about what I have to say.

But somewhere inside there is something that burns, has always burned; and there is a part of me that knows, in the most vague yet profound of ways, that this is a very important thing.

So this needs to be said, and so I will try to say it.

Every day I walk in off the Main and down the two short steps. The place is all post-industrial/nouveau bohemian hipster. Concrete walls and funky little tables. I stand at the doorway with my shoulder bag hanging across my chest and scope out the scene, looking for the best spot to grab a seat.

But it's all an act.

I thank the guy for the tall espresso and crack a few one-liners with him. I'm a regular here. Great coffee and cool tunes and the right kinda crowd. They know what's up. These people sitting around me, they could be my friends, could be my brethren.

But it never happens.

Because this is where I really want to be. Where I need to be. Sitting here alone, in the back of a café. Out here all on my own.

This is what monks used to do. Monks. These men of faith would give up all their worldly possessions and leave their comfortable lives, climbing to secluded mountaintops so they could be away from the world, alone and pure. In search of revelation, clarity, redemption.

That is me. Well, the revelation part for sure. Want that. Clarity too.

But I'm no monk. I don't take the easy road. I ain't soft like that. I don't cop out like those followers did. No way. I sit here right in the middle of it all. I don't run to the hills. I don't run from anything. Don't put it out of sight so that it can be out of mind. That would be too painless. No, I stay right here. A fake, a double agent, an active member and yet a constant reject – taking it in the face every fucking day.

Now *that's* sacrifice.

So I'm in the back corner of this café with my earphones on, hunched over my laptop. I blend right in. Nobody knows what I'm up to.

Sometimes when I'm feeling upbeat, or after a strong coffee, I'll tell myself that this is okay. That this is good. Not a waste of time at all. I will then feel inspired and motivated. I'll tell myself that this is about doing what you can. That it's about giving a shit. And how, if you break it down far enough, that is the only thing any of us can really do. The only way anything will change. Because we are both mother and child, cause and effect, villain and victim.

You see, I have gone underground. That's what all this is. Going on three-and-a-half years now.

Nobody knows exactly what I've been up to, just that I spend a lot of my free time in coffee shops "working on something."

It has been grueling. A marathon. And I am a tortoise. An insecure but passionate tortoise. Moving forward ever so slowly, hoping that sure and steady may one day win the race.

I have started and restarted a dozen times, deleted entire files, thrown out a full year of work in embarrassment and disgust. Living and rooting in my own filth, I have descended to very dark, very lonely places; telling myself that I am full of it and that I am trying wayyy too hard and that really, like who the hell do I think I am.

But still I persist.

Because I know now that there is nowhere else for me to go. Been there, done all that. No acting like nothing's wrong. No pretending that I'm cool with the way things are. No running and stumbling to any next stage.

So I sit here and fight the good fight.

Speak until one day I am heard.

Stand arms outstretched. Stare the sun down. Swallow poison. Scream my lungs out until it fills this room.

Even if it's in the dark. Even if I'm tucked far away in the back and nobody can hear me but me. Even if, in the end, it doesn't make much of a difference.

My story is becoming an old one. Went to school, got a diploma, got a job, and now, suddenly, here I am.

In my wallet I have a credit card with a balance that never seems to get any lower. If I go back far enough, if I call my credit card company and ask them for a summary, I will find the history of my last ten years, accruing interest.

Sometimes I walk around the city. I'll get myself excited about some errand I have to run – the video store, the pharmacy. I'll get dressed and then hit the streets, taking the long way, walking slowly around my neighborhood, pretending that I'm not secretly waiting and wishing for that certain something to happen. The way it does in the movies.

From the outside I look like any other guy.

After college I got a job and started working. This new career had absolutely nothing to do with my degree.

With the money from this job I leased a nice new car and thought it was really great. I paid my taxes and contributed to a retirement fund. Planned for my next vacation. Set up monthly bill payments to be automatically withdrawn from my account.

I did everything this next step said I was supposed to be doing and it felt good. Very adult.

And time passed.

Then one day, after a few years of driving my car to work and making payments and waiting for the weekends and going clubbing, I looked around at what was going on in my life and realized that I wasn't very excited about any of it.

Don't get me wrong, it was *okay*.

But then so is a sandwich.

Concerned, curious, I looked around some more. Around me I saw all my old friends from high school doing all the same stuff I was doing: living in the suburbs and going to the gym and driving nice new cars and having jobs and starting their lives and doing well for themselves – and not really giving a shit about any of it.

I could see it in their eyes. In the way they spoke.

My stomach began to wrench, a creeping feeling of unnamed dread that sank down deep. Then I looked around some more and saw my parents and your parents and their parents.

A mirror? A crystal ball?

A lifelong movie I already knew the ending to.

So I kinda freaked out. Nothing big, but enough. Something was definitely up and so I got the hell out of the suburbs and moved into the city. There I believed lay salvation.

I hooked up with an old friend of mine and we found a below-average apartment in a really cool part of town and made the move.

And then there we were. Living in the city.

Outside the doors of our apartment was the very heart of the city, pounding. Bright lights and night clubs, spray paint and street drama. Music escaping from everywhere. I walked around my new 'hood and let it all wash over me. Retro thrift shops. Hipster bars. Century-old kosher delis. The concrete dirty with ancient chewing gum and last night's debauchery and life being lived.

That wrenching feeling in my stomach began to fade, those daunting clouds looming up ahead began to disappear, and once again there were glimmers of possibility.

We got ourselves a few more friends and made ourselves a tight little crew. On sunny weekend afternoons our buddies played guitar in the park and I sat on the grass and read my books, the sounds of the city just a few feet away. At night we went to all the right bars and met all the right people and had some crazy times and everything was always a blur. Underground parties in industrial lofts. Happy hour on rooftops. Late night booty calls.

Walks of shame. In the winter we wasted time and dated people we didn't really like all that much, waiting for the summer to come once again so that we could walk the streets, and go to the festivals, and sit on terraces and enjoy the sun and every little bit of it all.

People would come to visit me, parents and cousins and old friends I would soon lose touch with. I was young and living in the cool part of town, doing that cool sort of thing, and they would all tell me how good I seemed to have it, how nice it must be.

I thanked them, and said yes, yes it was.

But sometimes there would be quiet moments – wandering around on a Sunday afternoon, eating dinner alone at my coffee table – when an old feeling that I thought was stilled would return.

The thought of what this might be quickly brought knots to my stomach. And it confused me. Why was it back? I couldn't understand where this was coming from. So I sat and contemplated and tried to figure out what it could be. I went down the list, checking off each part of my life, one by one.

It was all there. All of it. Right where it was supposed to be.

So I shrugged it off and went on with everything I was so busy doing, assuring myself that I was being silly, probably just an extra strong case of the lazy Sunday hangover blues. But as time went on, and the more that old shitty feeling reappeared, the harder and harder it got to ignore.

My friends, each in their own ways, were feeling the same. It was obvious. Whenever we had a quiet moment together we would eventually move toward more serious subjects. Like we were just waiting for the chance. It was always the same. We started under the guise of casual conversation, but then nimbly steered the talk where we needed it to go, each of us taking our turn, reviewing our lives, what was good and what was bad, and how of course I would rather this, would prefer that – but in all, everything was pretty good and going more or less accordingly to plan.

To get it off our chests.

To make sure it sounded right.

More time passed.

My friends and I all continued to do well. We moved on with our careers and began making our own way, out from our parents' shelter, walking down our own roads.

One began working on his PhD. Another opened his own restaurant. I started writing letters and opinion articles for the local newspaper, took some cool vacations, and finally paid off my car. Things were good.

And yet still it lingered.

I tried my best to deal with it. At first I would ignore it. Then try to reason with it. Make it into a joke. But to no avail; nothing worked. With each passing day that nameless cloud got bigger and bigger. It transformed from simply looming over my life into seeping down and becoming a permanent part of my every day.

An uninvited friend now relentlessly at my side. Always there with his two cents, constantly trying to mess with what I had going on.

Pretty soon I began seeing the dark side of every coin and finding some wrong in what I always assumed right. It was a serious bummer. My new companion was insistent, and intrusive, and insatiable. There was no reprieve, no shelter from his scrutiny. All was being judged and nobody would be let off the hook. Least of all me.

But I couldn't hate him. Could not dismiss him.

Because he was right, even if I was not wrong.

And then it started to get ugly.

Day-to-day life became a struggle and I was always the one caught in the middle. The simplest of social activities began requiring the greatest of efforts. I started to dread having to speak to anyone. The thought of polite chit-chat made me feel like I had to go to the bathroom. Only my closest friends gave me any sort of peace. Anything else was torture.

I avoided one-on-one situations, eye contact, and healthy relationships. Instead I took refuge in drinking too much, cheap sex, and sarcasm.

Unable to find secure ground in the present, I held onto the easiest parts of my past – and then took them too far.

I was at once in complete denial and completely aware of how I was handling things. And it pissed me off. You know, you try to do what you were taught was right, you try to fit in and get ahead and follow all the rules, you just wanna go on and live your life as best as you know how…but can't because you feel like a big fat fake. Because some part of you won't shut the fuck up.

Everything around me affirmed there was nothing else I could do – yet everything inside me cried that I was not doing enough.

Torn between what I saw and what I could not help but feel, frustrated at the daily void I couldn't stop tonguing, like the gap from a missing tooth, I became anxious and desperate. Again I felt the need to run, to stumble and stagger and seek deliverance. But I couldn't. I knew there was nowhere else for me to go, nowhere else for me to run to. I had arrived. Was already there.

I was stuck. I saw this. Had no choice but to accept it.

So to stay sane I did the only thing left to do. I held onto hope. Nameless, aimless hope.

I watched more movies and read more books. Always with some grand theme. A tragic love story. A critique of the status quo. A brave new world. A hero who dies.

I walked around the city constantly on the lookout, not knowing for what exactly but sure that it had to be there. An underground spirit mixed in with this daily grind. Some vibe that moved forward against the flow. A pocket of cool that burned fire and lived life and went on without me.

But I never found it. Or didn't know that I already had. Or wouldn't have recognized it anyway, not like that. And for a long while, that's just how things were.

On the streets after another night out.

It was a Saturday like a hundred others. I sat by the window, eating pizza, people-watching. And waiting.

Waiting.

I was very quickly reaching what seemed to be the end of the line. I was done searching in crowded bars and other people's beds. I could no longer drink it or shop it or fuck it away.

So as time passed and as the passion melted into impotence, into frustration, I simply took the next inevitable step – and began to hate. To hate all of this and everyone in it. Their clothes and cars and cell phones and stupid useless shit. All I could see was how much they wasted, how loud they laughed, how hard they tried…and how it was the same stuff I had been doing for so very long.

So with each night that passed, each day that was like yesterday, each month that became a year – ticking by, coasting along, wasting away – I felt the burning need to yell, to scream, to run into the street and grab strangers and shake them hard and ask them what the hell were they doing. Look at us. Look at all of this. Holy shit. DO SOMETHING! WILL SOMEONE FINALLY FUCKING DO SOMETHING?? Oh god please. Somebody. Something. Anything.

Please.

And so I ripped into the city and overdid it.

I didn't know what I was looking for and so I tried too hard. I didn't know what was missing and so expected too much.

I forever heard a clock ticking, as if time was running out, racing against a life I saw myself falling comfortably into. Moments, years, whatever. Constantly one step away from giving in, and saying okay, fine, you win – this is it.

My parents got divorced. I can still remember the day they told me.

I am six years old and standing in my bedroom. They are crouched over me, getting nice and close, explaining things to me the way you do to a young child. I barely register anything they say. All I can hear is the word. To a kid divorce brings on feelings of intense panic, even if you don't know exactly what it means. And then before you know it, it's over.

I was too young to remember much of anything else. Some tearful phone calls from my dad, who was a good guy but moved out of town to get his act together. My mother biting at her lower lip, worried and anxious but never showing it, making sure everything seemed as normal as possible. My little sister crying and frantic and asking why. And me, standing silent in the middle of it, watching our lives being flipped upside down and changed forever, quietly taking it all in, like a voyeur.

After my parents split, my mom and little sister and I moved into a basement apartment in a triplex in suburban Montreal. And we built our new life together. My mom was quiet and did what she had to, cutting coupons and stretching budgets and making sure that we always had what we needed. The scenes are still there for me to touch. My school lunch waiting for me on the kitchen counter each morning. A book from the library always beside her bed. An ironing board left standing open in front of the television. She was a humble hero of epic proportions and I will never be good enough to tell her story the way it deserves to be told. I love and miss her very much.

My grandparents were the best you could ask for, always there with food and family warmth. Most of my childhood memories come from their semi-detached house with the big balcony. My early years sprinkled with Yiddish and every stereotype you can imagine, and I really don't know how we would have turned out without the firm ground they laid under our feet.

That became my life and we went on with it. I was a good kid, causing some trouble but never crossing any lines. I looked very much like any other boy, going to school and playing sports and all that. I often overheard the adults commenting on how I was a nice, quiet kid. Maybe it was because I was the oldest. Maybe it was my way of helping out. I don't know. But I always felt the need to make sure that everything was all right, that things in my life weren't *that* bad. To accept what I had even if it wasn't ideal, so that we could go on as normally as possible. That was my thing. Still is in a lot of ways.

But on the inside, I often felt very different from my friends with their seemingly perfect lives and two parents and new cars and nice houses. Underneath my being so okay with it all, I was secretly ashamed of my separated family and low-income apartment and budget everything. I suppressed little bits of resentment toward all that I could not have. Toward the innocence taken from me too early. Toward all that was done by others and that I now had to live through.

What I didn't know at the time was that despite my feelings of martyrdom, I wasn't a unique or special victim. I was actually quite common, a living example of the newest trend – living in the suburbs and dealing with divorce.

You've seen the movies. At times it sucked pretty bad. As a young child I lived in the middle of a very messy marriage, watched my mother cry and cover her face. I sat on a bed in a dark bedroom and told my baby sister that it was okay, timing my words to cover the screams from down the hall. Learning at too young an age to lie, to ignore what you felt inside in order to make someone else feel better. I saw my mother work shitty jobs and struggle to raise two little kids on her own. Watched her search the city for deals on groceries after a long day's work, and dig her crappy car out of the snow, and go to bed alone. Every day. Every night.

But looking back now, and if given the chance today, I can't say that I would change much. Because it was a means to some end. I was able to experience first-hand how important it is to keep your family together, all while learning that some people just aren't made for each other. I got to watch a wonderfully simple woman, buried in the ordinary, accomplish the extraordinary. I developed a bond with my sibling that will never be broken. I became a young man, learned responsibility, humility.

And there were times, when the day was shining bright, that I felt that all of it – the complicated road, the ugly memories – had been just right. That somehow it had been meant to be. And in those brief moments, standing at my front door and staring out at my street, feeling the world open before me, I was sure of this very chaotic yet definite plan, one that had brought me through the years, through the ups and downs and harsh realities, to here, to me.

———

Like most kids I dreamed big dreams. My action figures always battled immeasurable odds and my last-minute shot always won the big game at the buzzer. Late at night, with the lights off and the covers over my head, I would lie in bed and continue the adventure, putting myself in the leading role and saving the day.

The years passed and the scenery began to change. I traded in my toys for movies and TV. Then one morning, the day after my twelfth birthday, I opened my eyes and saw something lying on my dresser. It had not been there when I'd gone to bed. I didn't know what it was and so got up and walked slowly over, trying not to get too freaked out. Standing there in my jammies, I stopped and stared at it, feeling that something mystical had happened while I'd slept.

Later on I discovered that my mom's friend had bought me that paperback book for my birthday and had placed it in my room during the night. That book ended up opening an amazing new door for me, one that still gives me hope and permission to dream.

Of course, today, I know that nothing magical really happened that night, just the coincidence of somebody choosing a book that happened to match my secret appetite for the epic.

But for a long time, whenever I thought of that day, I could feel worlds swirl around me.

———

The early 1990s.

History's awkward teenager. A time bordering two worlds, splitting the past from our present. The 80s – wacky and retro and linked to that flowered age we only saw in movies – would soon give way to today, progressed and obsessed and longing. In between were those early 90s. A time born at the end of the innocent old, soon to become the beginning of the informed new.

Threats of communism replaced by devotion to capitalism, cold wars by oil wars. Our desire for more grew big while our gadgets grew small. No longer did our phone calls have to wait for busy signals. Suddenly everything began appearing at our fingertips, and the entire world would soon be just a click away.

Glam rock and big hair gave way to grunge bands and suicides. Real hip-hop disappearing in all that bling. Tight stonewashed jeans became low and baggy, and we shopped in malls, and discovered the Internet, and drove around the suburbs.

I was your average teenager, neither too cool nor too lame. Instead my friends and I floated between the two, sticking close together and holding tightly onto our childhoods, moving in our own little bubble.

They were awkward years. My arms were too long and my sneakers too big. My hair was inescapably nappy and I overcompensated with way too much hair gel. Photographs from those years destined for future ridicule.

Grade school became junior high. As with every generation the styles floated in and out of our school, the day's latest fashions making their way through the corridors, spreading more out of social conformity than aesthetic merit. I can remember neon colors, and plaid lumberjack shirts, and acid wash finally fading away. Then came Doc Martens and the latest Air Jordan's. Calvin Klein underwear and those fancy five-ring spiral binders my mom could never afford.

The cultural identity that normally comes to define the spirit of a generation now coming from name brands we could buy, that you just had to have.

Was it always that way? Or were we the first?

Next I'm in high school, walking out of class.

Kids hang out by their lockers, waiting for the bell to ring between periods. The hustle and bustle of a high school hallway shows it all. Cool kids running in from their quick smokes, bullies acting like assholes, and girls ignoring classmates they used to be friends with. Some guy pulls up in a new car his daddy just bought him and instantly becomes a star.

A breeding ground for what is to come.

Cliques were formed and walls were put up. There was social segregation and prejudice. People's views of themselves and future measures of self-worth dictated by the insecurities of others.

Looking back, it is always that hallway I see – the long rows of lockers, those strange adolescent creatures huddled along the path ahead. Every morning I got up and got dressed and went to school, wading through this new landscape, interacting with the locals, and wondering what the hell was going on. I didn't recognize any of it.

The years went on. My voice deepened. Suddenly I had hair where there had been none before. I daydreamed through lectures and worried about my pimples and got nervous when I spoke to girls. I learned how to skip class and forge my mother's signature.

I moved along day to day, your everyday average kid.

And then, outta nowhere, you stop. And look around.

What was that?

Like when the refrigerator compressor all of a sudden stops humming. Or when the central air clicks off. A new, absolutely normal reality replaces the old, absolutely normal reality you were just in. Everything is exactly the same. Except…

An almost unnoticeable flicker. The slightest change in shade.

Everywhere.

Walking to the corner store. Sitting on the school bus, face pressed up against the window. At night in the back seat of my mom's car, driving through my life, sitting in darkness and watching my universe, the dark figures passing me by. All of it becoming somehow romantic, tragic.

Once upon a time the world had been nameless, always simply and safely mine. But now something had changed. My grade school's front lawn and those huge rust-red doors I had walked through each morning, now so tiny and unfamiliar in the glow of night. The cars parked along the streets of our neighborhood, the streets where we once roamed and reveled and raced our bikes. Now the cars had brand names, social status; now the streets had directions, led to destinations.

The familiar parts of my life suddenly viewed from a new perspective – classified, labeled, and precious only as longing memory.

My present now forced to compete with the past.

A sun creeping slowly up on the horizon, gently lighting up the morning sky. A new day. Your eyes adjust.

And eventually I began to see myself.

Suddenly worrying about shit I never knew existed. What I might look like if I walked down the school hallway alone. Those agonizing few seconds in the cafeteria before finding a perfect seat next to the perfect person. Wearing the wrong shirt.

Making people laugh at another kid's expense. Prejudging and poking fun just to make myself feel a bit better.

I noticed this evolution in myself. I observed and processed it. Again a voyeur.

The more the years went on, and the more time I spent trying to keep up and fit into this new world, the more I had to meld the person I had always been with the new version I saw myself becoming. And it was hard. I was a teenager growing up in a new reality, going along with what I was supposed to be going along with, but still I felt a strong connection to the boy I was leaving behind. I really liked him. I loved his big dreams and admired his high regard for himself and for what he believed he could accomplish, which knew no limits.

I knew that boy was still around. I could still hear his laugh.

Problem was that I was beginning to feel he was someone I used to know rather than someone I used to be.

My university was the kind you wanted to send your kids to. Beautiful old buildings and rolling hills, school spirit and football fields. It was everything you imagined a college campus to be.

I was roomed with three other guys in one of the newer dorms. A frantic mix of freshmen and pre-med, bongs and biology labs. Living on our own for the first time, we woke up late and crammed at last minutes and squeaked by classes. It rarely felt like school.

My college years were a blur. I played football and went to bars and got drunk and tried to get laid. That's about it. At the time it was all I wanted to do. All of it was new and intoxicating, and so for those years I didn't think about much of anything else.

I try to recall what else happened during that time and I come up with a blank. Well not a blank, but more like a collection of different pictures of the same stuff. The locations vary, the characters differ slightly, but it all looks pretty much the same.

Then one night I was sitting in the campus bar with my buddies, waiting to see what was gonna happen. The bar was typical, wooden booths and dim lights, and all around me kids wore school sweatshirts and shot pool. I was feeling a bit mellow that night. Maybe because it was a Tuesday, I don't remember, but I didn't have the energy to get excited about the usual. So I sat back and watched, something that's very much a part of my makeup but that I hadn't been doing much of lately.

The bar clamored on without me, a clutter of music and chatter and pinball machines. Above the bar one television was showing sports highlights and the other was replaying the nightly news. I watched the broadcasters' mouths move, saw the videos play and the headlines scroll. Outside of these doors, beyond the campus walls, the world went on without me.

It was the end of the 1990s and the century was almost over. We worried about Y2K and discovered Napster and summarized a millennium of human achievement in Top 10 lists and highlight reels.

I saw these big events, knew they were happening, but was too busy in this wonderland to have any of it sink in. Oh, that post-secondary bliss. Thousands and thousands of us in the twilight of our youth. Allowing us to play kid a little while longer, to keep the fun going for another four years.

A whole generation with student loans spent on food and drink. A whole generation with college degrees they don't really care about. I coasted through it all, doing what I had to, doing just enough to get by.

On the surface, on my surface, it was all good. I was having a blast. But underneath it something had begun to seep through. Inside a person there builds a natural accumulation of all that you have been doing, of all that you have been noticing, about the world around you, about yourself. And over time a vague, subconscious understanding begins to take place, coming in through the cracks. The scattered, nameless realizations eventually begin to form a picture, and the eternal process of discovery and then coping with what you've discovered rambles on.

On that night in that campus bar, I took a sip of my beer and tuned out for a bit. I sat quietly at a table and took a look around, recognizing the scene. A group of college boys acting like college boys. Girls pretending like they didn't care while they waited to be noticed. A bar full of students on a Tuesday night. They weren't doing anybody any harm, they were just out looking to have a good time.

But still I began to resent them.

I saw right through everything they were doing, and even though I couldn't precisely name what it was that I was hating, I hated it all the same. I felt both contempt for their ignorance – and a longing to join them once again. The first taste of the living paradox to come.

Given that I was the current captain of Team Typical Ignorant Fuck, this shedding of unfavorable light on my easy life should have been a huge bummer. But this time I did not shy away from the unpleasant thought. Didn't throw up any walls or try to unplug. I let it happen. I let myself not like where I was and what I was doing.

I needed to. If only for a moment. It felt good to take some time off from all the fun I was having.

My time at university eventually came to a close. It's almost the end now, a few days left to go. Another stage completed.

I was doing a bit better. Well, actually, that depends how you look at it. Better in the sense that I was no longer suppressing every uncomfortable thought that came to mind and pretending I hadn't heard what I had just thought? Yes.

But not better in terms of general daily contentment. No, not at all. Now I had become this big shot with myself, getting all deep, allowing bits of insight the chance to live, giving them some oxygen, letting them breathe, letting myself say what I had to say.

And so began the battle in my head. There I was and there they were, in a stare-down contest with myself. I was still a rookie at fucking with myself so it never lasted too long; I usually gave up pretty quickly. But even after I had buckled and blinked and slammed down the blinds and tried to tuck it all back away safe and sound – there the light remained. Lingering.

I was now dealing with uncharted territory, had officially left the nest, was no longer in blissful ignorance. All of that.

The beginning of the end or the end of the beginning. I was not sure. Still am not. But it definitely was the start of something that was unavoidable.

I walked through campus. I sat in the student center. Looked for seats in the library.

You nod hello to people you know. You ignore people you don't. You avoid faces you don't really feel like saying hi to. You go to classes chosen for convenient scheduling and sleeping in on Fridays. You skip the class. But that's okay because you download the lecture from the prof's website. You circle multiple-choice exams. You get your grades. You shrug that they're not that great. You still pass the class. You forget what you just learned.

There is more, of course. I know I am painting with a dark brush.

Still I cannot help it. Maybe I paint in dark because I know there should have been so much more light. I don't know. Maybe if the setting is bleak then the moment of redemption will be that much brighter.

Maybe it's because I wish I had been the hero, or at least half a hero. Or maybe I just wish that there had been more. That I had done more. And I am pissed there was not. That I was not.

Maybe I feel that it was somehow all wasted. That there should have been a moment, a perfectly scripted chain of events that led to a climax, a final center stage where all of us were together, gathered in one spot, and that a voice, preferably mine, began bellowing out all that we needed to hear. Taking us on a ride, a glorious, bullshit-breaking, tear-jerking ride. Uncovering lies we didn't know and calling out truths we too long chose to ignore. Preaching poetry, breathing fire.

Yes.

People suddenly forgetting where they were and what they had to do. That voice telling stories and drawing outlines, and everyone coming along and coloring them in, making their own pictures to the soundtrack.

All of them – friends and strangers and people who pass by one another every day. All of us – a generation beginning to realize that we knew too much for own good, too much for where we found ourselves headed.

Maybe they would begin to change. Maybe I would have changed.

Thousands of people suddenly moving in the same direction, as a whole but each on their own, following a long lost glimmer. Beginning to rise and drift far away. All the scared and beautiful pieces leading the way.

And in that brief moment nothing else would have mattered except what mattered most. And for a rare instant in an increasingly jaded blur, it would be very clear what that was.

Yes.

That's what I wish had happened.

But all that was years ago.

I'm living alone now. A nice place just a few blocks from the old bachelor pad. By now most of my friends have planted themselves in the city, fully emigrated from the burbs; back to the old inner-city neighbourhoods our immigrant grandparents once ran away from, gentrifying blocks and raising rents and re-stocking the ancient narrow streets and brown brick two-stories with trendy cafés and supper-clubs.

It's a nice night. I sit on my balcony and stare out at the streets, see the sidewalk scenes. Couples walk hand in hand. Headlights flash. It's a strange thing to pause for a moment and take a look at where you are in your life. Put it into words, say it out loud.

Below me the city moves and breathes. Tall buildings stand jagged and layered against the smooth evening sky, lined up as far as I can see, sprawled out so distant they make the horizon.

I stand up and lean against the rail of my balcony. Looking down on my street, below and to the left, I see the regulars hanging out in front of Harry's, the neighbourhood corner store. They smoke cigarettes and chat it up, standing beneath the flickering neon lights and worn-down beer ads. All kinds of different folk congregate on this corner, young and old, joking with Harry. They come and go. Come and go. Just hanging out.

I stand there alone on my balcony and watch these people smile and joke around, and I wonder where they live and what they do with the rest of their time. Where do they go when this is done? What are they laughing so easily about? What secrets do they possess?

I finished college, moved back in with my mom, got a job, moved to the city, started what I was supposed to be starting – and it was good.

Whenever the dreary reality of what I was doing with my life began to creep in and take the lustre off the numbingly correct steps I was in the middle of climbing, I simply jumped on to the next one, desperately in search of whatever it was that was lacking.

I've said all of this already.

From the burbs to the city, party to party, job to job, on and on.

For a while this did work, got me through the years and I had a good time. But it can really only go on for so long, running to the next stage in your life because you couldn't find what was missing in the last. Eventually there is nowhere left to go.

The alarm clock rings and I slap down hard on it, snoozing an extra ten minutes.

I get up and go to work. I finish work and have some dinner and try not to go to bed too late. Automatically racing from start to finish.

In between I have some fun. Watch TV. Go out and party. Feel shitty about it in the morning.

I'm guessing that my life is more or less like yours. I can't really complain. I have a decent job and a nice place to live. I have a solid group of friends and some girls here and there.

I am often content, occasionally happy, and most definitely not really that satisfied.

When I think back on my youth, my childhood seems to me a highlight reel of golden memories and long summer days. Never do I see the tedious times, the days spent wasting away in the classroom. Never do I think about the years of doing what I was told and loathing every minute of it – those things seemed to have never happened, not to me anyway.

Yesterday was nothing but good times, and today, well, I don't know.

But, what can you do?

I get up and go to work. I finish work and have some dinner and try not to go to bed too late. Automatically racing from start to finish.

Every part of my life passes me by and then grows in glory as the years build up over them. Each of my stages finishes, and then becomes sweeter than the reality they had actually been.

Sometimes I notice this and start to worry. And although the thought of this should be worrisome, my current state doesn't allow me to get overly excited about much of anything. So like a man casually contemplating the inevitable, I wonder if any of my presents will ever be as good as any of my pasts.

I can't remember how long this has been going on. There are no landmarks or points of reference. I'm always so surprised when people can remember their recent past with such detail – when they went there, what year they did that.

I work from home now. I get up and get dressed and brew my coffee and sit at my computer in my nice little office until five o'clock. Outside my window the sounds of the city keep me company.

After a while this becomes just like any other job, with my days morphing into their predecessors, and chunks of my life becoming indistinguishable from one another. I often forget what day of the week it is.

Of course I must be exaggerating.

When I was a kid I wanted to be an archaeologist, and an astronomer, and a baseball star. And then when called upon, when there was simply no one else, I would do my best to save the world.

Today my job is to find the cheapest shit possible.

Sure, I'm my own boss, and my position has a title and some prestige, and I write my emails very politely, but in the end – if you trim it all away and sum up my life's purpose for those forty hours a week – that is pretty much what you get.

I have all the chit-chat filler prepared for dinner parties and handshakes and so-what-do-you-do's. Sometimes I'll spice it up with words like "international" and "account manager." When pressed for further details, I am ready with explanations on how in today's global marketplace proper product sourcing and economies of scale can result in increased benefits for the end-consumer.

My grandmother used to skin dead chickens with her bare hands to feed the family. No joke. They literally ran from Nazis and nearly starved to death in the freezing forests of Poland and Russia. Lost like three quarters of their family. Then they came here and my grandfather hemmed pants for pennies a day. Fast forward a bit and see me being raised by a single mother on a low income.

All this to say that I am thankful for what I have. Okay? I am not some whiny, overprivileged, whatever you want to call it. I know how things can be. I grew up humble.

And therefore so what if I'm not exploring the heavens or saving the day? So what if I'm not rounding the bases and making the papers?

People want cheap T-shirts, the world needs to buy stuff for under a dollar, and so thank god for China. I know now that there is nothing wrong with this. We've all got to make a living somehow. I have told myself that it is acceptable to accept this.

Ours fathers would call it finally growing up.

I still go for drinks with my friends and lean against the bar and look around, packed into these places with other people looking around right back at me. It's so strange. There are so many of us. All of us doing this funny dance that we do. Well-dressed and perfectly in step and nobody leading.

It's been so long now. A lifetime has passed. Yet even after all these years, even with my perfected act and seamless mask, inside it still burns.

Because it is a shame. Such a shame.

Because I remember. Because I know what we really are.

Defused ticking time bombs. Idling supernova stars. Bottled lightning.

Of course that old, overwhelming feeling does come back now and then, and those dark, nameless clouds still sometimes loom. But it is different now. It doesn't freak me out anymore. No longer an intruding stranger that feels so foreign, but more like an estranged brother I cannot possibly turn away, no matter how often he knocks at my door. Somehow he always has a point that cannot be denied, and a button that he knows how to push; making me step back from the events in my life and feel dislocated, separated; looking back down at myself, as if I was not the one doing any of this.

I ask myself – is this a test?

I look around.

It has to be.

———

The restaurant is very chic. You walk in through the elegant glass doors and immediately it smacks you in the face. The music, the sexy lighting, the fancy people. The hostess is waiting for you, tall and blond and hot. She smiles and wears a very short skirt and walks you to the table. You smile back and say thank you and grab a seat. You're dressed up tonight and the music is bumping and you can't help but feel the vibe. You bob your head and look around, waiting for the other guests to arrive.

It's a birthday dinner like a hundred others you've probably been to. For some reason we love overpriced hotspots with faux-trendy decor and average food and ten-dollar drinks. We don't care if they pack us into long, uncomfortable tables or if the service is shit and the music is too loud to hear yourself think. Who needs to talk to their neighbor? This place is fucking hype!

It wears off fast. The demons begin to knock. And the dogs catch my scent. I look for a distraction, but my date is across from me squawking away with one of her friends. The seconds tick slowly by. After about twenty minutes I begin to get very antsy. I start drinking faster but am not enjoying it and not getting particularly drunk.

I try my best to socialize and make some wisecracks to the stranger sitting beside me, but after three minutes I've used up all my material and wonder what the hell I'm supposed to do next. My date is still engulfed in gossip, barely looking my way. Oh yes, this is just wonderful. Drag me out to a stranger's birthday dinner where I get to pay for an overpriced meal and sit for hours next to some guy I don't give two shits about (no offence, bro, I'm sure you are very nice person). I stare at her across from me. And the hate begins to build.

The night goes on, eternal. I'm taking deep gulps of beer now and my social skills are deteriorating. Finally the dinner ends, and as people begin to stand up from the table I disappear into the darkness and sneak off to the bar. I grab a spot and get busy with the task at hand. Don't judge me. I hand the bartender my credit card to show that I mean business.

Forty minutes later and the dinner tables get moved off to the sides and the restaurant gets very clubby, the music picking up speed. I am now a bit more than tipsy and looking for entertainment. So I move from group to group seeing what I can find. I'm a bobber and a weaver. In social situations like this I can't stay in one place for too long. In and out, in and out. I walk up to a group and listen to what her friends have to say, pretending to be interested – but am really just waiting for my chance to jump in and say something stupid, something clever yet ridiculous, and...wait for it...wait for it – here it is! Just dropped it in there without an invitation. Put it right out there. Bam, here you go, now deal with it. I giggle to myself. It's actually a pretty good one. I truly believe that they should like it, should love it even, but instead everyone pauses and just looks my way, like they don't really get it. It gets weird and eventually they turn and go back to what they were talking about.

Satisfied, I move on.

This is how I survive. Bottom-feeding off the secret ridicule of others and the finding of myself very funny. I'm that guy you don't know who shows up in the middle of your night out, standing there while you're just trying to have a good time, judging what you say and do, mentally noting that you're a fucking useless idiot.

I know, I know. I suck. I know all this hating of everything is very passé, very teenage angst. I'm also aware that it is a pathetically misanthropic cry for help – but until you come up with something better than this shit for a Saturday night in the prime of my life, well, this is what you're gonna get.

I shrug and order myself another drink.

———

The problem is in the changeovers. I guess it's the working from home during the day and the toiling in my own prison by night. So when the time comes to interact with the rest of the world, it's difficult to flick the switch on and jump back into this normal life as a normal guy. I get in so deep sometimes, so buried in all of this, and I am always so utterly alone, that when I have to make my way to the other side, into the light, well, I get a bit messed up in transit.

It's a juggling act. For my sanity I try to remain as ordinary as possible. Yet, also for my sanity, I need daily doses of hate and anger and outrage. It's a tough act to manage.

Scanning the latest news to find more ammunition, more targets. Devouring op-eds and old manifestos and then replaying them all in my head, regurgitating and updating and remixing. I'll be on a roll, replaying history, remaking our future – and then the phone will ring, or someone asks me to come out, and I have to snap out of it and quickly change my costume.

I'm like some sort of Clark Kent, and a conflicted and self-loathing wannabe of a Superman, trying to tuck his cape back into his pants so nobody notices what he's been up to.

So when the time comes to step out of my head and answer the day's call, to play my role in the normal world, I really have to rub at my eyes and gather myself. Wake up, boy. Snap out of it. Time to get 'er done! I take a deep breath and dive in.

At the café, ordering my coffee, and saying thank you to the waitress, and smiling a nice polite smile. But then there are dead, bloated bodies and so much suffering and rolling tanks and middle-aged white men in fancy suits – and I know that the look on my face betrays me.

Walking down the street with my head down, deep in my own thoughts. Step by step down the sidewalk I get deeper. I am really in a groove. In my head I am putting together pieces that will at once make love to the English language and change the world. But, up ahead, I see a casual acquaintance moving toward me. Suddenly the guy is upon me but I haven't had the time to snap out of it and switch over to normal guy mode, and now, to make things worse, he is trying to give me a fist bump instead of just shaking my hand. I am not prepared for this hip greeting and so don't handle it well, only partially making contact with his outstretched fist. It is very weak and extremely awkward. Normally I could recover, change the subject, laugh it off and smooth it out. But this time I don't. Can't. Because, well, because I don't really give a shit. Sorry, buddy. It's not you, it's me. How could I really be expected to care? Not with what I know.

At a bar I sit with some friends around a table and we're having a few pints. It's a cool night at a cool place. The music rocks and the beer flows and the talk gets louder. Things are good tonight, we're all having a blast. But suddenly I notice that I am noticing that it is good rather than just enjoying the goodness. Shit. I tell my brain to shut up, to just go with it. Don't mess this up. Not again. But as the time passes I see myself starting. It's subtle at first. Bit by bit. Shifting the subject, directing the talk, trying to get people where I need them to be. With me. Please, please, come with me. And before I know it I am talking a bit too loud, getting a bit too passionate, bringing up subjects that are a bit too serious – and the conversation loses its flow. It's no big deal, the night goes on and nobody notices. But I do. I know that I have done it again.

Clark Kent had his nerdy act, bumping into things and adjusting his glasses. He was good at it. And he knew it, you could see it in that little smirk of his. He was able to manage the charade and deal with the inner conflict because he knew what he really was and what he could really do. Sure, he was alone, and never got any credit, but he knew, in the end, that he could indeed save the world. All he needed was a bit of time and a kiss from Lois Lane.

So yeah, I can relate. It must have been tough for Clark to keep up that everyday act while he really had the power of the sun burning inside him, having to let Lois think he was a putz when he really could have ripped off his shirt and blown her socks and skirt off.

I too have a secret identity. I too burn with an innate belief that I am meant for something more, for something big and beautiful.

But I stop there. That is as far as I'll go with the comparison. Because no matter how epic I wish my story was, no matter how much I suffer and struggle and hope, I know that Superman was not this much of a pussy.

The guy serving me is dressed pretty funky. Skinny jeans with a silver studded belt. I could never pull this off. Do you know how stupid I would look? I have to be very careful with how cool I try to dress; anything that deviates too much from the center just doesn't work on me. I've always envied guys like this. Dudes who could bust out these outfits and get trendy haircuts. I've never had a cool haircut. Ever. The history of me and hair goes from unmanageable, nappy curls on my head to unauthorized new residence on my back.

But what can you do?

Every day I walk in off the main and down the two short steps. The place is all post-industrial/nouveau bohemian hipster. Concrete walls and funky little tables. I stand at the doorway with my urban shoulder bag hanging across my chest and scope out the scene, looking for the best spot to grab a seat.

But it's all an act.

Because this is where I really want to be. Where I need to be. Sitting here alone, in the back of a café. Out here all on my own.

You see, I have gone underground. That's what all this is. Going on five years now.

It has been grueling. I have started and restarted a dozen times.

But still I persist.

Because I know that there is nowhere else for me to go. Been there, done all that. No acting like nothing's wrong. No pretending that I'm cool with the way things are. No running and stumbling to any next stage.

So I begin to stand and fight the good fight.

Even if it's in the dark. Even if I'm tucked far away in the back and nobody can hear me but me. Even if, in the end, it doesn't make much of a difference.

Blink. And one-and-a-half acres of rainforest are cut down. Every second of every day. Go to bed. And 150 species are driven to extinction. Gone forever.

Step outside and a million cars are idling.
Step on the gas pedal and a billion more tons are rising.
Wade in traffic and pump what you must and pay what you are told.

And tomorrow it happens all over again.

Bits and pieces fly by. In newspapers and documentaries and dinner conversations. Four hundred million dollars spent by oil companies to lobby the right politicians. Millions more to deny global warming and lull us into inaction. The warmest eight years ever recorded occurring in the last decade. An electric car killed and secretly taken off the roads. City buses in Norway running on hydrogen and emitting nothing from their tailpipes but drinkable water.

You see it too. A president with seven of his cabinet members coming from the oil and energy industry. Iraq having the world's third largest oil reserves. An oil company posting $40.6 billion in profits, the most by a U.S. company in history. Freedom as justification for invasion and occupation.

Oh yes, you see it all. Dead civilians, and grieving mothers, and a whole new generation of extreme hate. Bombs dropping. Homes destroyed. Soldiers with their faces melted off.

But then a horn honks and the phone rings and it's time to go.

While we eat breakfast and prepare dinner, multinational pharmaceutical companies push for changes to international law so that poor nations must buy their brand-name HIV/AIDS medication instead of the cheaper generic versions made in Brazil or India. Some can afford the brand-name versions, most cannot. And people die.

Desperate third-world countries are given aid money by the World Bank and the IMF, but only if they agree to open their borders for drilling and mining and privatization of their industries. The results are often devastating. Poor nations end up owing rich nations impossible sums of money, the debt mounts higher, interest payments cripple their already impoverished economies. Modern slavery disguised as foreign aid. And people suffer.

The global economy is pushed to the edge of depression by greed and an unhealthy, hyper-capitalist system. Entire countries dive into deep financial distress, millions of workers are fired from their jobs, people lose their life savings, their homes – and the system and those who perpetuate it just keep on going. And nothing changes.

Brave leaders in oppressed countries jailed for speaking their minds. Cowardly leaders in free countries re-elected to office. Industry spokespeople and pundits with prepared statements repeating talking points that get them through the interview and allow all of this to go on and on and on. Money is made. Status quo continues.

And we see this.

It all happens right in front of our faces. Being absorbed. Swallowed.

Then, when our guard is down, there comes a moment when the grave reality and consequence of it all slips in and hits us. We stop what we are doing. Puzzle pieces begin to come together. For a split second we let ourselves see what is really going on and where it all comes from. Our stomachs begin to burn. In sadness and in rage and in shame. And for that instant we can feel the true pain, the unbelievable anguish, multiplying by the dozens, the hundreds, thousands, millions.

I turn on the TV and wait for what I see to match what I know.

Global spending on the military over $1.5 trillion dollars per year. Over two billion children on the planet Earth, 1 billion of them living in poverty.

But it never comes.

Thirty thousand kids under the age of five dying every day, enough to fill a stadium.

One billion people without clean water, living in diseased filth.

The world's three richest *people* having more money than the poorest forty-eight *countries* combined.

It never ever comes.

Instead corruption and suffering exist only as passing sound bites. Celebrity divorce is today's top news.

So I change the channel and try to go on with my day. But it's getting harder and harder.

The United Nations tells me that less than $20 is needed to feed a starving person for a year. Forbes tells me that McDonald's revenue is more than $63 million a day.

Every year Americans spend $154 billion on Christmas gifts, $1.9 billion more on Easter candy. Every day thirty-five million of their fellow US citizens, including twelve million children, go hungry.

If there is such a thing as a soul, surely ours is crying.

The channel changes again. On comes a press conference with people standing in front of flags that wave, repeating words now diminished. Polluting companies painting themselves green while they turn the sky black. Wars waged and drilling pushed into law and billions and billions more dollars going to the top.

Next we stop for a commercial break. Flashing bright colors turn kids into good little consumers. Teams of marketers use manufactured stars to define what we should think is cool.

I see what I should wear, how I should look, and which beers will get me into mansions full of babes.

I see it.

That we spend hundreds of billions of dollars on fake plastic toys and designer jeans and cell phones; the waste and dyes from their assembly-line production pouring into our rivers; the energy needed to make us these cultural necessities burning black smoke into our air.

That we've created a $50 billion bottled-water industry to keep us safe from all our self-inflicted ills, a trendy plastic Band-Aid that lets us go blissfully on with what we are doing, but one that burns more oil and heats more atmosphere and buries more synthetic garbage in our soils.

That in the middle of the Pacific Ocean, not too far from Hawaii, floats a mass of plastic. It heaves up and down with the movement of the waves, like some science-fiction creature, sucking in everything around it. Millions of tons of garbage, stuff we bought and then threw away, eventually made its way down sewers and along rivers and out to the open sea; the ocean currents taking it all along, until it gathered with more floating trash, year after year, swirling together like a spiral galaxy, coalescing, growing. Dolphins and sea turtles have been found dead in the middle of this synthetic island, the insides of their stomachs lined with old plastic shopping bags, their throats gagged shut with our rotting consumer garbage. This mass of toxic debris floating in our ocean is now bigger than the state of Texas, bigger than all of France.

I see it all.

The green lungs and lifeblood of our planet cut down to graze cheeseburgers and fuel SUVs. The sheets of glacial ice the size of New York breaking off and raising our seas. The big boxes where we shop for our food, efficiently grown with millions of tons of chemical fertilizers that seep toxins into our soil and run lethal pollutants into our water.

That cancer rates over the last thirty years have increased by more than 50 percent, and are expected to increase by another 50 percent in the next twenty years.

That my mother died.

That I have nowhere else to go but here.

That no matter how much I try to change the channel I can't help but still see this, can't help but still be a part of it.

So I switch off the TV.

But will turn it back on tomorrow.

———

That nameless cloud that used to haunt me? Yeah, finally it has a name.

And that's part of the problem. For so long there was "something" bothering me, making me feel unsettled and unsatisfied. The origin of my malaise had always been nameless, unidentified, and so my angst was general, unarticulated. As the years went on and as more and more somethings had to be witnessed and lived through and accepted, my inability to define the source of what was bothering me led to severe frustration and – with no specific target for my grievances – a growing disdain for just about everything.

That was what I was dealing with. A deep and innate sense that the things around you are very, very wrong, mixed with the dawning realization that you are not only a part of it, but that this life road you find yourself on offers no alternative destination.

This can be very frightening. You panic. You desperately want to jump off this train and change all your directions – but cannot, do not. Why? Because even if you know down deep to your core that you should seriously reconsider what you and we have been doing, even if you feel that it is beyond a shadow of a doubt the right thing to do…unfortunately it is usually too late. You have already begun to teeter. Between the raw arrogance of youth, and the practical compromising of adulthood. Between naturally believing that you can do anything, and sensibly rationalizing that sometimes you just cannot.

You are caught. In limbo. In the purgatory between child and adult. In that torturous stage where you still have beautiful young eyes and start to see that you are not using them as you once did.

So, feeling frustrated and powerless, you lash out, become petulant, throw punches in the dark.

I did a lot of that.

Then one day, after enough time has passed and enough books are read, after you have seen enough documentaries that shed light, enough evil bullshit that drives you mad – you begin to see a bit more clearly. The bigger picture begins to form. You can see not only what the greater puzzle is, but how and why its pieces fit together. *The source of your sorrow is no longer a mystery.* You can finally identify the culprits. The causes of the world's problems, of your problems, are finally identifiable. Aha! The bad guys, caught red-handed.

At first this seemed like a very important event. I felt relieved. I knew whom and what to hate.

But very quickly I began to realize that this breakthrough was not necessarily good news.

Every day more and more truths were being revealed to me. With or without my consent. I became very skilled at seeing behind the surface. Behind every surface. But as with one of those grainy collage paintings where you can only see the hidden image after adjusting the way you look at it, it became difficult to stop seeing this once I had started.

So yes, I can now name some names and quote some numbers, but as time goes on I see that my angst is not relieved, my anger not assuaged.

If anything I feel more surrounded, more squeezed, into this lonely corner. Sure I can now point fingers, but when there are so many things to point at that you don't know where to start pointing – are you really any better off?

I don't know. It doesn't feel that way right now. Now my frustrations simply have more ammo, more doors to knock on and names to call out. The evil is now everywhere. And I can't stop seeing it.

In the job I have, the car I drive, the food I eat, the products I buy, music I hear, TV I watch, very life that I am living.

I can't go to a movie without leaning into my friend and whispering/regurgitating a social commentary. I can no longer cheer for any professional sport because I see how greed and market forces have created ridiculously high salaries and ticket prices that alienate all but the rich and corrupt athletes and take the joy out of the games we once loved. I can't read the newspaper without seeing beyond the fluffy headline. Can't hear a politician speak without immediately hearing the ulterior motive. Can't shop without regretting my part in our consumer culture. Can't drive to the suburbs without noticing the urban sprawl. Can't walk by a car without tasting the heat rising to our skies. Can't even take a break and unplug from all of this without feeling guilty for unplugging.

Because I can now see it all. And cannot stop seeing it. Waste and mental distortion in every part of our culture. A hundred destroyed villages in every gallon of gas. A thousand clear-cut acres in every Big Mac. A million dead bodies for every day I allow this to go on…

So yes, now I know whom to hate. And no, I do not feel any better about it.

All that this mad scramble for discovery and understanding has accomplished is to have chopped away at that many more simple pleasures, causing me to feel more and more detached from the norms, isolated from the masses, and critical of just about everything.

Here I am. Finally aware. Finally articulate in what it is that has been haunting me. Finally.

Yet after all this time, after finally reaching this goal, I feel that it doesn't really matter. Not one bit.

Because despite all that I feel, all that I now know…there is not a damn thing I can do about any of it.

Years ago the answer came to me.

I was sitting at the park with my buddies, the mountain and the angelic grey statue overlooking the boulevard, and we were picking at the grass, taking some sun, and talking about life the way only hungover twenty-somethings can. What we wanted, what we regretted, what was missing. Blah blah blah.

Everything around me still affirmed there was nothing else I could do, yet everything inside me still cried that I was not doing enough. It was eternal.

And then it hit me.

There must be more.

We need more.

That was it. Right at that moment I knew that was it. No words had ever sounded truer. It was the burning flame, the restless stir, the indescribable haunting the soul.

And then it was over. Just like that. We walked back home and continued on with our day and I did whatever it is that normal people do – but this time carrying the maddeningly impossible burden of returning to earth and pretending that the universe had not just been opened before me.

We need more. That super-simple statement started a half-decade-long inquiry that is still a big fat mess in my head. But, despite my augmented daily anguish, at least I now had two points to work with. Sort of a starting and ending point:

We are unsatisfied----------We need more

Actually, there are probably three points needed:
We were once happy--------We are now unsatisfied---------We need more

No, wait, there are four:
We were once happy----------We are now unsatisfied---------We need more----------So what the hell do we do about it?

Initially I did try to tackle all four points at once and screwed myself up. Screwed myself up big time. I started this adventure by spending three years concocting an elaborate fictional story that would 1) revisit my wonderful childhood innocence, 2) describe the difficult years as I felt that innocence begin to disappear, 3) lament how today is super shitty (personal life and world entire), 4) discover and present real-life solutions to solve all the world's problems (and in turn, my own), and 5) wrap it all up in a nail-biting drama and epic love story.

Tucked away in my PC is a folder labeled with a clever name, and in that folder lie the rejects. The graveyard of an amateur's ambition. Dozens of drafts very similar to what you have been reading but dressed up in hundreds of pages of "story." They have many of the same events and ideas, the same passion and purpose, but are wrapped in a shell of fiction, supposedly so that

I could better engage the reader and personalize the issues. Maybe if I built a story that connected with people, one with some tragedy and love and drama, then I could more profoundly present the serious issues that I felt needed to be dealt with, both globally and personally. It did not work. I was speaking from the heart but not in my own voice. And I was taking on way too much. I could not even figure out my own day-to-day real life, let alone my real life altered to fit into a complex fictional world with character development, story arc, poverty reduction, and social revolution. It was becoming a big disaster. So scared and insecure was I to simply speak my mind as me that I wound up neck-deep in evil multinational corporations, Robin Hood-style computer theft, millions of dollars for feeding the poor, and the world somehow having its eyes blasted opened by our brave and noble actions. By the end there was even a Euro-looking assassin after us. It was crazy. I was working on this monster every day, fully aware that it didn't feel right, didn't sound honest. It wasn't until I got some sound advice from a special person that I gathered the guts to shed the elaborate fiction and just speak as me, which was what this whole thing was about to begin with.

So having already been thoroughly humbled by taking on more than I should, I will start with the first three points, nice and simple, and see if that gets me any farther:

We were once happy----------We are now unsatisfied----------We need more

We were once happy. We've already done the past. Once upon a time you were young and things were all good. Despite whatever curveballs life threw at you, you somehow just knew that things would always be okay. You know how it was. You are a kid and full of hope and life is simple, so you can deal with whatever comes your way. It doesn't matter what happens because you still believe, still truly believe, that those big dreams of yours will come true someday. When you're a child, the horizons are all endless and so there is plenty of room to dream. Inside all of us there is a tipping point, a dividing line. And while you are on one side of this divide, everything can be seen in color, any ugly event can be swallowed and still be painted bright – because you are still there, still in it, still swimming in the full half of the glass.

We are now unsatisfied. My fall into dissatisfaction has been described in great detail. It was a downward spiral that took many years to reach bottom. It began with a slow, gradual opening of the eyes…and then quickly accelerated with each year that passed. Eventually you end up at today and are more than properly jaded. I have listed a bunch of reasons why we are unhappy with the present state of the world and our lives, have listed the names and numbers and could go on listing a million more. But right now the specifics don't matter as much as the overall picture – time passes, you grow up, and those horizons no longer seem endless. Actually, all the roads around us start to look like they are leading in the same direction, and if the shit we have been seeing lately is an example of where these roads will end up, if this is what our future will hold, then, no kidding, we start to feel anxious about things. And as the years go on and as you see more and more crap, it gets harder to hold onto that old hopefulness of youth. The protective armour around your childlike spirit gets chipped at, bit by bit, and you get dangerously close to that tipping point. You creep right up to that dividing line. It is a dangerous time, because once you cross that line, once too much of you gets held back, used up, forced to accept – then life's possibilities begin to seem like inevitabilities, and the cup you are swimming in no longer feels half full. It now starts to feel sorta empty. And so everything begins to feel sorta empty. Too much of what you used to have inside you has been swallowed. And buried. And politely asked to grow up. You have officially crossed over the line and the color of things changes. A scar is left on your innocent eyes, a wound that takes longer and longer to heal each time life pokes at it; and regardless how much time passes or how hard you try to see in those old colors again, you can never get all the way back to where you once were. Trading magic for fact, no trade backs.

We need more: Great. Could I be any more vague? We need more. We need more. For a long time I sat on that little kernel of revelation like a mother chicken sitting on her eggs – an angry, frustrated mother chicken, screaming down at her unborn babies, "Come on! I know you're in there. Hatch already. I need some fucking answers!" It was a difficult time. I have already recounted the years spent in purgatory. The battle with the voices and the looming clouds over my daily life. But slowly, as I read and watched and tried to hold on and give a shit, one by one the pieces of the puzzle I so desperately needed did start to come to life. Little bits of observation and insight popping in my head.

Hundreds of useless thoughts were aborted, but some of my offspring survived, and were accepted into the dysfunctional family of my mind with open arms. I did my best to nurture them and give them what they needed to grow. Sometimes it was ugly, and incestuous, but other times it was very beautiful. And for me, absolutely necessary (and without getting too far ahead of myself, absolutely necessary for all of us).

If the ultimate goal of all this is the alleviation of dissatisfaction and arrival at a deeper sense of personal happiness, then the simple naming of names is not really a solution. Or even a breakthrough. It is merely a step. A required part of the process that will in all likelihood cause more angst and anger, not less. Painful but necessary.

So having finally taken a step back and divided the big mess into things we can more easily see, more easily manage, we can now get a bit more focused and properly ask: what is the more that we need?

With the walls crumbling down all around us and our lives tick-tocking away, this is our natural inclination. To try to find a solution as fast as possible. What are the problems, here are some solutions that make sense, now let's do this shit.

But no. I have learned from my mistakes. Step by step, please.

We need to reduce things down a bit further. We should not be asking *what* is it that we need, but *why* do we need it? *Why do we need more?* Why amid all this plenty do we feel that something is missing?

That is the question that needs some answering. And for that we need a different perspective, one that is distanced from all these modern conventions we consider gospel. A stroll through the generations. As a preamble. A research assignment. A look at where we came from in order to understand where we are now.

———

A bit of history.

Before 1950 the world was really a very different place. Human history up to that point had been marked by difficult daily lives and very few luxuries, with most people struggling just to get through their day. Then came World War II and all those years of tragedy, so when the 50s finally came along the world desperately needed to rebuild and regenerate. And a new era began. Peace had arrived and people could finally relax and start to focus on themselves. The war was won, evil was defeated, and the American Dream, and all those on the side of it, prospered. Factories stopped making bullets and tanks and started producing refrigerators and TVs. Color TVs! Within a few years the suburbs were fully settled and nice new cars were bought. People of this generation were the firstborn children of the new modern age, and they had plenty to keep themselves occupied. Everything was so new, so modern. And there was so much of it all. Corporations expanded, marketing and advertising blossomed, and it all rolled along so beautifully. Before you knew it every house had a car and a television and people absolutely loved it. An age of consumerism began and it was as American as apple pie. Things were really swell. You could see it in the music. The 1950s was the golden age of mainstream rock 'n' roll. This new genre of music definitely rocked some conservative old boats but in reality, revolutionary or not, the rock music of that era was still pretty light and easy. Of course an underground counterculture was pushing things forward, but I'm talking about the mainstream music scene and the general mood of the moment. Times were good, war was over, industry was booming, and people were happy with what they had. No matter Elvis's scandalous gyrations, the mainstream culture was still innocent and it did not take much to keep people satisfied. The majority of music reflected this. Simple lyrics, simple beats, just wanna rock around the clock and kiss my girl and dance that little dance.

Then the 1960s started and cracks in this shiny new world began to show. As prosperity settled across western nations, more and more people started to travel the globe, go to college, learn about the world, and step outside of their bubble. And the innocence began to fade. The years went on and suddenly, in the midst of all this perfectly marketed Americana, were hippies asking for peace and blacks asking for equal rights. For so many years "happiness" had been achieved by simply moving up the ladder and keeping up with the wonders of technology; but now the realities of the world were beginning to seep into kitchens and living rooms, opening eyes and raising the bar of personal satisfaction. The image of the smiling housewife and the shiny new car was replaced by demonstrations at schools, riots in the streets, and marches with a million men.

It was not because those who came of age in the 60s and 70s were any smarter or braver then their parents, it was simply a matter of education and evolution. They were no longer children of a new modern age, but adolescents, growing and learning about what was happening around them. And the more they saw – the more television and courageous journalists and college campuses showed them – the more they felt that all was not groovy. They could no longer sit in front of the TV with their parents and blissfully watch Ed Sullivan. Humans have an innate desire to progress, there is no escaping it, so with their everyday lives now nice and comfortable and stable, and with more education than their parents, the baby boomers needed something more than what had satisfied their parents. With an immoral war in Vietnam, a moral fight for civil rights, and kids trying to move past the cultural close-mindedness of the previous generation, the fault lines under society began to shift. Cultures clashed. The future called, the past resisted, and you could literally see the new pushing against the old.

Today I cannot imagine any of us giving up even a day of our rat race to march for what we felt was right. But they did it. The 1960s turned into the 70s and still they took to the streets, defied their parents, changed their clothing, their hair, and forced a new direction. The effects were felt everywhere. Fluff persisted of course, but was marginalized. Movies became more gritty. Mainstream music became a bit heavier, a bit darker. Billboard hits were no longer full of mindless fun; now the most popular songs had deeper lyrics and were laced with social commentary. The Times They Were A-Changing and people were looking for answers Blowing in the Wind. Artists tapped into what they were feeling as individuals and into what society was feeling as a whole, no longer content with the same old shit, no longer able to ignore what was going on around them. They began playing harder, riffing on electric instead of acoustic, rebelling with their words and guitars until they let out what was raging inside, until they were spent, overdosed, dead. Revolution and Vietnam and Woodstock and Watergate and the major issues of the day on everybody's lips. The world watched as the adolescents of the modern world voiced their displeasure, demanding a different future.

I still listen to Dylan and Baez and CCR and Cat Stevens and imagine a whole generation feeling as if they were fighting for what was right, that they were working toward something new, something big – and how wonderful that must have been. Feeling that they were breaking from the restrictive past, breaking so far from it that they could create a new direction, not only for themselves but for the world. And they almost did it.

But then the 80s happened. And that fire began to die. Well not die, it never dies, it just gets buried. In this case buried under flashy, cheap electro, neon-lit 1980s distraction. How did we go from barefoot, peace-loving hippies to polyester, slick-haired douchebags? From standing at the gates of a complete cultural revolution to the apex of cheap materialism – in just a few years? I don't know. A new decade began, and suddenly the protests against what was wrong and the fights in the streets for what was right were forgotten. Instead of following up on the momentum of the movement, instead of actually living that new future they had marched for, we let it all just fade away. Why? Maybe they were tired. Maybe it was all the drama and unrest lived during the 60s and 70s that allowed the 80s to become so easily distracted. Maybe they needed a break. Maybe they had seen that all that anger and revolution and standing up to the man hadn't really gotten them anywhere. Pointless wars were still waged, thousands upon thousands still died, and human greed still found ways to do what it wanted. So maybe the 80s just wanted to unplug after decades of so much hard work that didn't really get us anywhere. Maybe that's why they immersed themselves so easily in MTV and Wall Street and overconsumption. Maybe that's why they built more shopping malls than schools. Why the movies were so painfully cheesy. Why the music moved from thoughtful, powerful classics to mindless glam rock. It's as if they purposely tried to remove any thought from everything. Song lyrics became full of "Domo Arigato Mr. Roboto" and "Everybody Wang Chung Tonight." An underground punk movement existed, but it did not affect the masses. The hard rockers that made it to the mainstream weren't really that hard; instead of blazing new paths and rocking the establishment, they teased their hair and wore eyeliner. As a society we returned to the good old ways of acquiring material wealth as a pursuit of happiness. Returned to it with a vengeance (because maybe that would help us forget). New gadgets invaded from Japan and we welcomed them in, buying Walkmans and VHS recorders and immersing ourselves once again in all the wondrous technology. With each passing year the money flowed faster and our need for more grew and we pumped out more sitcoms and cartoons and complementary merchandise. TV ruled like never before, and a new generation of eager consumers were bamboozled into believing that pop culture was the only culture. Period. Ronald Reagan and his friends made sure it all grew and grew until the American Consumer Dream returned not only as a way of life, but as a brand that could not be denied. Financial markets expanded and began to dominate. Corporations forced politicians toward deregulation and began wielding unheard-of influence. Lamborghinis and big-tittied blondes became symbols of success. Looking back, everything was so big and flashy and over the top and almost purposefully brainless. As if we were overcompensating. As if we were trying so very, very hard.

And when we put our minds to something, man, do we do it well. The effects of our devotion to consumption-based capitalism reached everywhere, across oceans and into other countries, shining like some glamorous beacon of prosperity. From culture to business to government policy and all the way into the next generation.

The 1980s came to an end. The 1990s arrived. But this decade did not revolt against its predecessor in the way the 60s revolted against the 50s. No. We took that stonewashed, shoulder-pad-wearing 1980s dream and kept it going. The style changed a bit, hip hop began to influence the mainstream, but the underlying shallow zeitgeist was still there. You could see it in the ridiculous outfits and bright colors and stupid haircuts, like we were still playing dress-up. Oh yeah, we kept it going all right. Technological advance after technological advance wowed us and kept us in awe. Cassette to CD. VHS to DVD. Video games evolved from block figures shifting side to side to all-encompassing digital worlds we could disappear into. Personal computers entered the home and we were never going to be the same. We dug deeper and deeper into consumer culture, not only living as consumers but building our lives around what we consumed. Cell phones, laptops, MP3s. Now there were new ways to communicate, to learn, to exist. Our old addiction to buying things coincided perfectly with this new way to live. The self-perpetuating circle of market/sell/buy–market/sell/buy no longer had to convince people that they needed this or that because we were making these luxury products a literal necessity in our lives. It was a capitalist match made in heaven.

Yet as we were living in this digital/material world of the 1990s, another phenomenon was also taking place. We were going to school more than any other generation in history. High school was now a prerequisite, not a final destination. Going to college was the new norm. "Higher education," with all its faults, still forced us to see more of the world. To sit with other students from other walks of life and discuss things like international relations and religion and Intro to Metaphysics. A universe of higher thinking our parents never even put a foot into. Even if we didn't pay much attention to it, even if we forgot most of what we had learned, it was still there, inside us. The door now opened just a bit.

And not only did we learn more, but we also lived *with* more than ever before. Our surroundings evolved. New immigrants to our cities changed from the standard light-skinned Irish, Jews, and Italians to darker, more exotic varieties. Suddenly the kids in our classes were black and brown and yellow. Suddenly they were our neighbors and girlfriends and boyfriends. And it was completely normal to us. Different ethnicity, different religions – the biggest hurdles and causes of strife in the history of the world – almost gone in a generation. I fooled around with a veritable United Nations of girls in my day and didn't think a thing of it. It was all good baby baby. That hurdle, that cultural mind-block that had held back the progress of society throughout the history of humankind was no longer in our way. We were open. Open to the world like never before.

Now add to this all the information we could suddenly access through computers and the Internet, and not only were the societal borders of the world disappearing, but also the physical. By the late 1990s we could instantly learn about everything our planet had to offer. Every day the number of websites grew exponentially, some completely useless but others offering the knowledge of the world to us on a silicon platter. We began to develop a sense of omnipotence. A surface, shallow, fleeting omnipotence; but still, we could literally know anything and be anywhere.

Furthermore, the rampant materialism of the 80s and 90s had fueled easy money and created a culture of debt, so now kids could finish school, get a credit card or credit line, and travel the world entire. Just like that. Without a thought. Pick a place on the map and hop on a plane and backpack through it. Have all the comforts of home with you as you cash advanced from an ATM outside of the Parthenon or on an island in Thailand. Without missing a thing, without breaking a sweat. The final barriers of the world gone. Nothing was beyond us now.

This was amazing. Well, it should have been amazing. Being the most educated, knowledgeable, capable generation in history, we should have, theoretically, also been the happiest. But we were not. Despite all the wonders we were blessed with, we were living in the most reclusive, compartmentalized, jaded, dreamless environment ever. Knowing so much and having access to almost anything, yet – at the core – still feeling unsatisfied, still feeling like there was nothing for us to do and nowhere special to end up. A maddening paradox of so much potential power living in a time of such institutionalized powerlessness.

And once again you could see it in the music. A new genre crept out from underneath all this, one that spoke to the unspoken emotions of the generation. Grunge or alternative rock was born from the same burning spirit as jazz and rock 'n' roll and punk. After more than a decade of society living in all that fluff, a deep-seated disenchantment was quietly growing and passive-aggressively began to leak out into our music. The musicians labeled as grunge could not specifically define our feelings of powerlessness, yet they were still filled with rage over it. They hated the void we felt inside and did their best to make sure we didn't ignore its existence. But unlike the music of the 60s that called out what was wrong and suggested a better way forward, the grunge rockers of the 90s knew that things were off but felt there was nothing they could do about it. Fake Plastic Trees and Smells Like Teen Spirit. We were depressed, and angry, and wished for change; but did not know exactly why or exactly how. The music perfectly expressed these underlying, anonymous feelings. There was beauty in it, the heartbreaking beauty of a restless soul, but it only went so far. Instead of attacking the root causes or demanding a new direction, it passionately lamented the emptiness up ahead, pissed off at where they were headed and that they were the ones taking themselves there. They were dark poets trying to sound an alarm. And as of today, the last of their kind.

But the people of the 90s did not reject the material world inherited from the 80s. No no, they kept it going and updated it for a new decade. Found new ways to integrate themselves further into this way of life.

Times were good. Consumer culture continued to explode. Mega-movies and flashy colors dominated. Money flowed and dot.com bubbles grew.

But underneath the surface of all this "progress" people continued to feel dissatisfied, unfulfilled, and apathetic – and cracks finally began to form. That's where that hard music and beautifully depressing lyrics came from, and why it was broadly accepted. This frustration with the direction of our lives built up in the underground at first, and when it finally began to leak into the mainstream it connected powerfully with the youth of the generation. The young always express what the masses are secretly feeling. That's why millions upon millions of Pearl Jam, Nirvana, Radiohead, and Tool records were sold. The lament for our modern fate was felt by everyone, even if it was only the hard rockers and teenagers who had the balls to say it out loud.

Yet despite the long-haired vanguards screaming their lungs out, despite the millions of fans bringing their worries into the mainstream, for some reason that's where it ended. The cries of displeasure were out there, on the radio stations and billboard charts and lips of our youth for everyone to hear – but did not catch on any deeper into the general culture. Not like they did in previous generations. Those old 60s and 70s calls for peace and love and revolution made it into the mainstream and then spread all the way across the masses and into the top layer of the cultural debate, right out in the open. But that's not what happened in the 90s. We felt that nameless cloud, we secretly agreed with those who spoke and sang about it, but we did not take it any further. We simply let those vital gut feelings slip down into the lower levels of our priorities. Buried. And then we just went on with things.

This continues today.

We of the new millennium are anything but new. We are but a slightly more advanced version of what we were in the 90s. Not a new creation, not a new cultural direction, just an upgrade of the same old model. Generation 2.0. The 80s turned into the 90s and the 90s turned into today. Four decades in a row without a major cultural upheaval. The same old trends have continued:

technology intertwines itself in our lives a little more every day, consumerism is still the most dominant religion, mainstream culture remains mindless.

I will now quote myself from a few pages ago. I don't know if that's weird or not.

"Being the most educated, knowledgeable, capable generation in history, we should have, theoretically, also been the happiest. But we were not. Despite all the wonders we were blessed with, we were living in the most reclusive, compartmentalized, jaded, dreamless environment ever."

Decades later and everything is still the same. It has simply gone on and on. There has been no revolution, no revolt.

So if we felt dissatisfied and unfulfilled and trapped in a heart-shaped box back in the 90s – imagine now.

Today we continue to go to school in record numbers, have access to information like never before, and can so easily accomplish what once seemed impossible. With each minute that passes we make the world that much smaller. Today we can shrink it down so small, everything we have ever known, every nation every name every fact – all of it compressed and zipped and downloaded onto our laptops and phones, at our fingertips faster and faster every day. Our omnipotence grows. Each day we become more powerful, more all-knowing. Our world becomes less impressive, easier to access, cheaper to own.

And at the same time the cultural walls we began to break down in the 90s are almost completely gone today. Forget the right-wing crazies and Islamophobes, the majority of us normal people continue to integrate with and accept into our lives new and different perspectives each and everyday. My Jewish bubby has accepted my goyishe girlfriend. An African-American man with the middle name Hussein was elected president of the United States.

On a personal level, we continue to progress, continue to grow in wisdom and in capability – yet our cultural surroundings stay the same. Our day-to-day culture is not evolving along with us. We grow bigger and bigger as the room we must sit in stays fixed.

Dissatisfaction is inevitable.

"A maddening paradox of so much potential power living in a time of such institutionalized powerlessness."

This is where we are today.

And so I wonder: if suppressed dissatisfaction about the state of the world and their place in it drove some people of the 90s to sad lyrics and suicides, what will happen to us when what we bury becomes too much to bear?

I don't know. I look for signs around me today but can't find a thing.

We don't grow our hair long or act all angst-y. We don't rage against the machine or smash pumpkins. Agree with the melancholy style of 1990s rockers or not, at least it was a passionate expression, a cry in the dark. At least they created something raw and beautiful out of love and giving of a shit.

Today there doesn't seem to be even the slightest bit of frustration or disenchantment in our mainstream culture. No cry of displeasure from our youth, not in a way that has broken through to the masses. We don't get angry. We don't lament.

So as a member of today, I pose the question: as our generation quietly becomes intolerably full with how much we swallow, as today's secret discontent grows yet everything stays the same – what are we doing about it?

———

I step outside my front door and smell the fresh autumn air. The trees are almost completely stripped down now, the burnt red and orange colors gone, only yellow leaves left hanging on. I walk down the steps outside of my new condo, by the nice little gardens on each side of the walkway, and onto the sidewalk of my new neighborhood.

I've moved to another part of town. Still a cool area, but a bit quieter, a bit more refined. Now when I look down from my balcony I see couples pushing strollers and walking their dogs.

I always liked to think that I never followed the usual steps everybody else did, that I would forever be doing my own thing. The young kid playing with the big boys, the old guy at the bar. But with each passing year I realize that this perception of myself is actually not that accurate. Just look at me now, getting tired of the late nights, taking it easy with the stupid shit, and changing neighborhoods to follow age and income. Seems I have been following the common path for quite some time now.

The part of me that considers himself of a revolutionary will fight this of course, will continue to contest and struggle for some chaos, but down deep I am already sort of accepting my fate. And am cool with it. My friends are now having babies, and moving back to the suburbs to find a house with a backyard, and have stopped wondering about when their secret dreams will start to come true. Finally leaving the last pieces of childhood behind. And I am en route to do the same. Am one step away from drinking the inevitable, comfortable Kool-Aid.

And somewhere a voice is telling me, *You see, I told you so*.

I can critique and fight it as much as I want and it won't make much of a difference. The days go by and I see that life cares not a bit about my musings. And so I would concede, would accept defeat and throw my hands up in surrender, admit it was all just the impetuous ambitions of youth.

But I can't.

Maybe I'm stubborn. Still a bit immature. Maybe a part of me just isn't ready to completely let go. Or maybe a part of me still knows that I never should.

Whatever it is, here I still am, at a coffee shop, sitting with my earphones on, hunched over my laptop.

I look down at my screen and try to focus, rereading a few pages from my last session, revising and touching up, like a sort of warm-up. Around me the walls are decorated old-fashioned rustic, splashed with some hipster cool, meant for a slightly older but still with-it crowd. It's a small place with great coffee and awesome people and a nice neighborhood feel. The guy behind the counter works the big red espresso machine and schmoozes with the regulars.

This is my new spot, in my new stage in life, and most of the time it's all very normal. We work during the day, see our friends on the weekends, and visit with our families as much as we can. We are moving forward the way people do. Now people are talking about kids. Biological clocks are ticking. We get together with couples for dinner. Bring bottles of wine instead of six-packs of beer.

On the weekends we wake up early and shop for home décor and talk about real estate and how much should we really spend on this duvet.

This stage has bestowed upon me some new and pretty heavy responsibilities. A mortgage. Paying off those credit cards. Everything now purchased for two. These days I worry about things I never worried about before. My health. Providing for someone other than me. What sort of future my family will have.

Everyday I move farther up the common road. And as I move along it – as I stop at each stop and actually see the sights, experience the daily comings and goings – I see that it is not as frightening as I had imagined it. There is not some ugly future looming up ahead that I desperately need to avoid. No train that I must jump off. Time passes and I see that this is what people do and that it is okay for this to be your life. Go to work, build a nice family, come home and watch the game. Nothing wrong with that.

This is what I am doing. Things are going well and I am happy. And if I was to come to the end of my road and have nothing to show for it but a life kindly lived and a loving family by my side – wouldn't that be enough? Yes, it probably would be. In the end it is pretty much all that anybody can ask for, all that anyone really needs.

But unfortunately I know that it will not do.

That cloud I used to see looming up ahead had been a warning bell, a metaphor for what I saw was changing. The lowering ceiling on youth's infinite dreams. The end to once endless horizons. Back then, in those wonder years, I could see this change coming. Looking up ahead from my place in childhood I could clearly see the difference between what I was feeling in my young heart and what I saw happening in the future. I could see this difference because I still had one foot in the past, was still seeing with young eyes.

But today I am almost completely living in the present. With both feet in. I see no more ominous clouds looming because after enough time under a new sky you no longer notice any difference. You are simply in it and that is all you can see.

Living today in this nice comfortable life and knowing that there is nothing wrong with it; but also knowing that there had once been another view of today, one that was also right and powerful and pure, and much more suspect of this present state. Another paradox to deal with, thank you very much.

So when I sneak off into this corner of the café and turn on my laptop, when I step away from my everyday normal life to try to slip back to the past, looking for old colors, I begin to feel a bit unsure about what I am doing. I look around and everywhere are signs of this normal life I should be living. Doubt starts to seep in. Insecurity begins to play its games. Where I used to feel like Clark Kent trying to juggle two identities, now it's more like a husband feeling that he's neglecting his duties for some secret second life.

I try to brush it off and tell myself its okay. I try to shake off the demons of self-doubt and keep the faith that I am doing the right thing. But it's nearly impossible to do. I am in the middle of examining the deepest of my own feelings, stuck in the inescapable momentum of present becoming future, trying to reconcile past memories with current realities.

And if I am wrong, if all this work is off, or just plain sucks and I have indeed been wasting all this time, all these years, when I could have been doing something else, something more productive, like everyone else seems to be doing…

I know, I know, I shouldn't think this way. But it's hard. Every day that passes I get farther and farther away from that boy I used to know and closer and closer to the man I will end up as. I just hope that I will always remember something I used to believe very strongly – that one does not have to erase the other.

Late at night, and I gently close the front door of my condo behind me.

I put my shoes on and move quietly down the stairs. Down in the basement of my building, among the concrete walls, I flip on the light outside of my storage room. I open up the scuffed-up white door and start to move crap around. I make a big mess, digging for that one box obviously all the way at the bottom of the pile.

Finally I find it. Rip it open, for some reason very desperate to get my hands on what is inside.

I bend over and swipe away some papers, digging some more until I see it. The familiar artwork, the old, ragged corners. These books are the ones I felt compelled to keep as part of my very humble permanent collection, kept with me through all the years and moves. I remove some of the classics, discover some long forgotten gems, and smile at the old Stephen King that kept me dreaming big. I dig a bit deeper, pick out four or five more, and sigh in relief.

For the last few days I have been feeling stuck. Not so much with writer's block, writing was not the issue, it was more like I had dug myself too deep. I feel this way when I get too far away from the everyday me, too deep into the oh so very serious. Although there is a part of me that knows I have been doing some good stuff, if I go on for too long I begin to feel detached from the surface. Spending too much time perfecting your own thoughts can leave you feeling very distanced from reality. And when I get too deep, too far from the real world, the slightest hiccup can start a chain reaction of unhealthy thinking. You are on a roll, page after page, thoughts finally coming together, leading you deeper and deeper – but then suddenly there's a bump and something snaps you out of your little universe. You look around. How long was I gone? You get nervous. You scramble to get back to the zone, back to where you had just been. But when you cannot return to that magical place quickly enough, when the thoughts no longer flow and you feel that every attempt to restart sounds so full of shit, your mind begins to wander. The real world starts to seep in. Can everybody see what I have been up to? Do they know? Yes, they know. They know the truth. They can see. You start to feel silly. The demons begin their feast.

It can get ugly. Now mix this ravenous self-consciousness with the realities of my life today – a family, a career I am trying to build, responsibilities I feel hanging over my head – and now the guilt really starts to flow. If people knew – my clients, my father, my friends with their normal lives – if they knew all the hours, all the hundreds, the thousands of hours, of me sitting here and contemplating, searching and searching for god knows what…

And that is why I am here in the basement of my building in the middle of the night, on my knees, head buried in an old dusty box. To find some backup. Some reassurance that all this well-intentioned but very abstract work indeed has a place in the real world I must live in.

Thoreau living in the woods outside of Walden. Chuck Palahniuk and Tyler Durden trying to tear it all down. Kazantzakis reporting on the life he's lived, trying his best to leave nothing but an empty bag of bones.

To see some of those big dreams again. To be reminded that it's okay. To be given permission once more.

I close up the box and lock the storage room door. I walk back up the stairs and try not to make any noise. Everybody in the building is asleep. Cradling the old books in my arms I lock my front door behind me and tiptoe into my bedroom. It is dark. The only light coming from my back balcony, glowing through the curtains. I lie silently in bed and wait for sleep, knowing that it will come soon. The old companions are now piled beside me on my night table. I may or may not reread them. But it doesn't really matter, I know that they're there.

―――

Expressions that have made it through the years, sayings that have held true – about it being the journey and not the destination, about the satisfaction from hard work, the road less traveled – these come from somewhere and mean something.

We human beings are meant to struggle, to reach higher, to discover and achieve and explore. Read our ancient stories, think of the movies we love, the songs that move us. All of them speak in some way to that indefinable human need for something more.

Where does this come from?

Maybe it's just our egos. Maybe it's how we give praise to this unimaginably beautiful world we find ourselves randomly living in. Or maybe it's our only real way to try and get closer to the divine.

Whatever the source of this upward urge – we are meant to reach higher. Make no mistake. That is who we are.

Our ancestors had to hunt their own meat, plough their own fields, and fight just to survive – the most primal of satisfactions. They did not contemplate their existence; they were too busy making it from scratch. If they were warm and healthy and fed, they were happy.

Our great-grandparents worked day and night in a new world, doing what they had to in order to support their families and move them forward – a noble and lifelong struggle. Look at how they stand in old portraits and black and white photographs. Backs straight. Simple yet proud.

Our grandparents kept busy worrying about world wars and building a good home and holding onto humble jobs and putting food on the table. Then the times changed and they pushed our parents to get an education and go to college, the first time in history that the majority could worry about such luxuries.

Then came us. Today. And all of a sudden there is nothing left to do. Not in that deeply fulfilling way we humans need.

Because today everything we in the West could possibly need is already at our fingertips. Everything pre-packed and disposable, just sitting there and waiting for us. Today our survival is a given. Clean water magically flowing, food piled high in endless rows. A mother does not have to worry about feeding her child. A father is no longer necessary for his family to be provided for.

We do not have to struggle to fulfill our basic human needs, so there is no satisfaction when they are achieved. Simply living no longer feels like anything special.

And with the achievement of our basic needs already automatically pre-installed for us, we, in that eternal human drive for more, naturally move on to the "higher" pursuits of modern society, still looking for that deeper personal satisfaction.

Go to university. Get a degree. See the world.

Done, done, and done. We just breezed through what used to be the highest of our higher pursuits and I barely broke a sweat.

So what now? How do I attain fulfillment? What is there left for me to do? Nothing. Because we want for nothing. And it is so easy. The shoes I'm wearing right now cost more than what two billion people in the world earn for months of backbreaking work, and I coasted through a few hours in a bullshit job to get them.

I throw out what others die for. I am fat and satiated and do not know where to turn to next. I roam through today looking for someplace to stretch my wings. In vain. My flames have nowhere to burn, my passion nothing to conquer. I drive-thru, not climb, my mountains.

I take a deep long look at my life and wonder – what have I ever fought for, struggled to get, even worked that hard to earn?

I have trouble finding an answer.

Today it is not only our most basic needs that are a given, not only society's highest achievements that come to us so easily – but all the world's wonders, the planet's most lavish luxuries, the latest and the best, all that we could ever dream of. Just a pre-approved monthly payment away.

We have it all. We have it all and more. And because it is so easy to get, having it doesn't really satisfy us.

I have dined in China and wandered through the streets of Europe and flown over the Arctic. I have driven by families living in horrible slums, and flown over the Grand Canyon at twenty thousand feet. I have climbed a volcano in the middle of the Mediterranean, raved with thousands under a full moon, and lain on Roman marble in an ancient Turkish bath.

It reads like an adventure, a life fully lived. And so does yours. But still, to our generation, all of these amazing moments are simply backstory in our seemingly very common lives. Fleeting memories. No big deal. Just another part of another day.

Why? Why are we, who have so much, so perpetually dissatisfied? Because we need more. And because what we are doing today is not enough. That is the why.

We are blessed, no doubt, and I wish I could just sit back and shut up and enjoy all of this. I really do. But I can't. It just doesn't happen.

Something weighs on me. That old friend of mine, echoes of our past, whispered calls to greatness.

When all the possibilities, all the wonders you can ever hope to discover, are too casually reached – by drifting through school, working some job you don't care about – when all the things you can possibly hope to accomplish in your life are too easily attained, the day will inevitably come when those once endless horizons are all finally reached, and still you will be left wanting.

———

So there is a void, a dark and cosmic gap, between what we need as humans beings living in this peak of human history and what we have been doing to satisfy this need.

It is this difference between what we need and what we do that leaves us feeling like something is missing. It calls to us, this void. It makes us feel unsettled, not at peace.

But then life beckons and we must go along with it. We try our best day to day. We do what we must. And we end up not having the time to bother with that old emptiness floating around. So it gets buried. Yet whether we realize it or not, it is always there, and we are constantly dealing with it. Subconsciously trying to fix the problem, feel better, fill that space.

People will always try to fill the void.

Unfortunately we're going about it all wrong.

I look at what we are doing today like a father desperately heartbroken over what has become of his son's life. Unable to stop him from wasting it all away, unable to forget the potential, the light that once shined. And I am both the father and the son.

I am surrounded and I am overwhelmed. By how badly we want to be veiled. How easily we accept illusions. How little we demand of ourselves.

In an era when all our needs are already satisfied, when we can so easily get what we want when we want it, you would think that in our innate human quest for "more" we would naturally gravitate to something other than this, something more…significant.

But we don't.

In a time when we know how our planet moves and breathes, when children have access to limitless amounts of information, and adults can grasp the intricate problems facing our civilization, we continue to produce entire generations that do not seek any sort of higher path for their lives.

No. Instead we revel in the banal. We obsess about the trivial. We spend our time on this earth playing make-believe, content to pretend that we do not know what is happening right in front of us. And then we scratch our heads and wonder why something doesn't feel right.

We have absolutely no idea what we really want, what we really need; and so like spoiled little children unable to articulate what is actually bothering us, we throw our new toys to the side, desperately grasp for the next distraction, and then stomp our feet and sulk when we are left still unsatisfied.

It's really quite embarrassing.

We are social creatures. As much as we are fiercely independent, so are we dependent. People have always longed for acceptance by others in their society, from the jungle tribe to the village community to the individual in the big city. We shape how we live our lives based on this need. We look at where we are and try to adapt, to fit in, to move forward within our circumstances.

But what happens when the ideals we humans are expected to live by are no longer based in humanity? What happens when we seek approval from a society whose values are no longer good for us?

The lines become blurred. And we get lost in between.

The hypercapitalist mentality that currently dominates the planet's economic and commercial systems may or may not be a good way to run a world, but that is another argument for another day. The more personal and pressing problem is that this commercial way of living, like the appetite of any beast, has grown out of control. The capitalist ideology that emerged victorious during this past century has now left the realm of theory and industry and spilled over into almost every aspect of our personal lives, literally changing the way we live, changing the ways we think. Changing our value systems.

New rules for a new world. Everything in our lives has been transformed to keep up with this reality: our jobs, our technology, what we teach and how we learn.

Only one thing has stayed essentially the same.

Us.

As much as we try to adapt and fit in to this modern capitalist society, we are, at our cores, exactly who we have always been. And we were not made for this.

Yet from the day we are born we are raised in the middle of a bizarre consumer culture, learning to be consumers before we learn to be anything else. The average two-year-old can recognize approximately twenty corporate brands before he or she learns to speak.

The contradictions begin. Who we are versus what we are given.

Still, we have no choice but to go on. So looking to move forward within our circumstances, looking to feel accepted in the world we find ourselves living in, we start to accept new definitions, definitions given to us by a commercialized society – efficient, immutable, mechanical – and are told to make them our own.

The average person in a western nation gets bombarded by approximately three thousand marketing messages per day. Globally, companies now spend over one trillion dollars per year on advertising to convince us of what we are better off buying. That we are missing something. That this or that material thing will make our lives better.

Without even realizing it, we have integrated these new definitions into our ethos, into our way of seeing things. We have accepted a new, foreign perception of value. An entire culture now believing that the pursuit of material wealth equals the pursuit of happiness.

And we wander on, forever looking for that something that is missing, doing the best we can with what we are given. But it's not natural. We are not meant for this. People with hopes and fears and hearts and souls expected to be fulfilled in a system made for the disposable.

Looking for peace while living in this conflict, constantly ramming together puzzle pieces that do not fit.

It may or may not be our fault, but the fact remains, we are doing all the wrong things.

When surveyed the majority of people today describe "success" not in terms of personal growth or building of a family or cultural progress, but as some sort of material or financial gain.

When surveyed the majority of people admit to not feeling a high level of satisfaction with their lives.

Television, movies, fashion magazines. Ads on every street corner/ newspaper /radio/webpage, reminding women that there are ways to be prettier, slimmer, happier. Just flip the page, recognize this brand, change yourself. Two thirds of women admit to wanting to alter their bodies with some sort of cosmetic procedure. Tens of millions of women suffer from serious eating disorders.

Billions of dollars per year spent on marketing useless products and junk food directly to young children. Companies consult child psychologists to find the optimal colors, sounds, and other stimuli that will most effectively deliver their commercial message to the developing minds of our youth. The five-to-fourteen year old age group is now the most sought after marketing segment of our population. Music videos contain approximately ninety-three sexual situations per hour. While both parents go to work to be able to pay for the products we now believe we need, the average kid spends almost forty hours per week alone looking at some sort of screen – TV, telephone, video game, computer – absorbing every bit. Approximately one million young children in North America are now diagnosed and on medication for social anxiety disorders.

Men are told their heads are too bald and their penises too limp. It is suggested that I might have new name-brand conditions like "Low T" (low testosterone) and "ED" (erectile dysfunction). These newly discovered illnesses are often advertised during newly discovered holidays: Propetia Boxing Day Bonanza, Viagra Black Friday Fiesta. A bit depressed? Life not feeling the way it used to? Don't step away from your cubicle and traffic jam to get some fresh air or spend time with the family; don't put down that remote control and pick up a book – nah, just go to the mall and renew your prescription and pick it up at the drive-thru pharmacy as you update your status on Facebook.

And when the buzz wears off, after we have stuffed our faces and popped the pills and finished shopping, when that same feeling of purposelessness reappears, now deeper and more gaping…

We change the channel and look for more. More. Doing what we have been taught.

On flashes *Survivor*, *Big Brother*, *Jersey Shore*, *The Gold-Digging Real Housewives of Who the Fuck Cares*, and a hundred other "realities". Paris Hilton, Kim Kardashian, and whoever happens to be the current next thing. Random people becoming rich and famous for no apparent reason. Hundreds of paparazzi, thousands of flashing cameras. Scrambling on top of each other, rolling around like jackals for a scrap of food.

This is what happens when people and values become commercialized. A consumer culture is a celebrity culture, and in such a world these are the new gods.

Someone makes a catchy tune, finds a new way to act like an idiot, or gives a blowjob on camera, and suddenly the divine dream of celebrity has come true. Just like that.

Look at them, we social creatures say. Look at these famous people. They have it all. They have what we have been told we need. They are getting the attention of the whole society. Fully accepted. Adored. At the top of our cultural mountain. The mountain we've been taught we must climb.

More and more and more. The fantasy continues, becomes even more warped, digs itself deeper into our psyche.

Life is kinda tough. Things don't feel like they used to. For some reason I am not satisfied with what I am doing, with what I have.

Maybe if I'm famous and have all that stuff then I will feel happy, like they seem to be.

God willing.

I once saw this kid trying out for *American Idol*. He waited for hours and hours, standing in an endless line with thousands of other hopefuls. He was then herded into a crowded waiting room to sit and anxiously wait for his chance. Finally he got his big audition – and was swiftly but politely rejected by the judges. Interviewed outside the audition room the boy, nearly a full grown adult male, was in tears, inconsolable, sobbing like he'd just lost a loved one in a horrible accident. The only words I could make out through his frantic misery were not about his love of music; instead he repeated over and over, "I, I, I, just want to be famous…"

On *The Bachelor* and *The Bachelorette* television shows, grown men and women declare love for people they've just met, giving the most sacred part of themselves up in some sick hybrid of finding love and competing to be the "winner." When they are not chosen to move onto the next level of the competition, and they start to cry, so very very disappointed, I wonder: are they sad because they've lost their chance at true love, or because they've lost their chance at being famous?

The deep personal fulfillment people once searched for in the love from another human being – now interchangeable, now having the same value, as a few minutes of fleeting fame.

Paris Hilton, world-famous for having fucked some guy on camera and for her daddy being very rich, got caught drinking and driving one night and was put into a county jail for a few days. The day of her release hundreds of reporters staked out the area and waited anxiously at her house. Helicopters flew above to get video of her car moving down the street. The coverage of this monumental event dominated the news cycle. CNN, supposedly the most balanced source of news on American cable television, had a timer at the bottom of their screen counting down the hours until the socialite's appearance on *Larry King Live* that night. The gold-coloured clock ticked down second after second throughout CNN's primetime lineup, hypnotizing the audience, making it seem that this absolutely meaningless event was worth planning a whole evening around. It was one of the show's highest rated episodes of the year.

After the oil runs out and the oceans rise and we kill one another in a panic to survive, future historians will use this to explain what went wrong.

Imagine receiving a birthday or Christmas gift from a friend. You hunker down, all excited, and open up the box. And there sits a homemade present. Not bought from a store, but made at home by your friend's own two hands. For nine out of ten of us the first thought would be, *What the fuck is this?* That would be our natural reaction. We would not think about that friend spending countless hours of their personal time, using raw materials purchased with their hard-earned dollars, agonizing over every little detail with the sole purpose of making you happy, of creating something for you out of genuine thoughtfulness and care. No. This homemade gift would have little or no value to us. It would be considered a joke, something to be embarrassed by and gossiped about.

But open that same box and see a sweater with the right brand name on it and we are instantly satisfied. No matter that it was most likely bought at the last minute off the rack at some mall. No matter that it was probably made in a Bangladeshi shithole factory by workers living near poverty and that we will only wear it a handful of times. Still we smile. Feel comfort. This has value to us.

Where does this distorted sense of value come from? The commercialization of everything. People, the environment, and now even our sense of worth. This commercialization has blurred the lines between the material world and the people who must live in it.

Can we see it in the music? Don't even get me started. I haven't listened to the radio in years. Our mainstream music makes me very worried about the fate of our civilization. The capitalist/consumer way of thinking has taken over even the arts, with everything now pre-planned and manufactured. If some silly song randomly becomes successful, one hundred clones are immediately sent out into the public to jump on the new wave, no matter if it is of no artistic value and degrades our culture. And like good little children, we buy what we are sold.

Our generation's continued embrace of the cheap and frivolous has fed the beast and created a commercial situation where only something with a catchy beat and reference to partying or sex will make it to the masses. Hey, I like my fun music as much as the next guy, and I don't mind that there is an industry that sells it to us, but when the children of our generation have nothing to choose from but "Poker Face" or "I Kissed a Girl and I Liked It," when the only lyrics that play in the earphones of our youth are about money and cars and being slutty, then I think there is a serious problem.

Bob Dylan once topped the billboard charts. Simon & Garfunkel were true musicians creating truly beautiful music. Even the 80s had its share of quality stuff that made it across the mainstream. And the 90s produced the last best rock we have seen to date.

Today we have pretty faces and empty lyrics. A Katie Perry record was nominated for Album of the Year at the Grammys (the Grammys, not the MTV Music Awards).

Where is the quality in our mainstream? I don't know. It's becoming very hard to find. It seems we now piece together a cultural identity based on successful bits of the past, no longer able to create anything new of our own, never having learned that trick. So we regurgitate old styles. Bring back the 80s and 90s even though they've just ended. Our movies are remakes of what was once popular; our music is remixed from what was once cool.

Think about the musical/cultural revolutions of the past and what they added to our history: Miles Davis and the jazz greats laying the base for future genres of music while fighting through unbelievable racism. Hendrix and Joplin and Dylan and a whole generation making music that broke down society's old walls. House DJs and independent electro artists producing beauty in a digital world, creating a new universe of eclectic electronic music. All of these were artistic creations that added positively to the culture *and* were commercially successful across the mainstream.

Now think about what this latest generation has added to the global catalogue.

Yeah. Exactly.

I'm not exaggerating just to make a point. The quality of music available in our mainstream (as just one example) perfectly represents the overall state of our culture. It is laced with materialism and vanity, the crafty salesmen of a consumer culture. And a consumer culture is also a disposable culture, so what is produced within it will be just that: glaringly cheap and instantly replaceable.

And it's all connected. Since we have had no choice but to grow up in this, we have, intentionally or not, made this our new value system. Those are the values we have been taught, this is what we continue to accept, and so that is what is given to us.

Like a vicious circle, the things that we do to find some satisfaction are the very things that cause our dissatisfaction. Over and over and over, spilling into all aspects of our lives.

A newer car. A bigger TV. The holiday season transformed into the shopping season. Anxious, panicked; lined up around the corner, waiting for the doors to open. To fill our faces, our homes, our closets, this burning need.

iPhones to replace our iPhones. A $300 pair of jeans. The hottest brand name. Generation after generation, millions of us, with the world at our fingertips, the power to do almost anything, knowing that there is so much wrong that needs to be set right – choosing careers based on starting salary instead of passion, becoming hedge-fund managers instead of doctors, working jobs we hate to buy shit we don't need.

Giving ourselves away so easily.

Feeding the deepest of our needs the shallowest of things.

And so we remain constantly searching. Never satisfied. Only pacified.

Not too long ago we were raised with a different definition of success. A different definition of value. Work hard and earn the good things in life; but also aim to be an upstanding member of your community, and, as a guiding principle in our lives, try your best to always do the right thing. A healthy mix of individualism and humanity.

There was, once upon a time, a strong moral foundation to almost everything we did. From the college professor to the factory worker, we all understood that there were some things that could not be easily measured. That living by your principles was more valuable than any superficial achievements. Actually, personal pursuits based purely on money and status were once looked down upon by society, perceived as, and not in line with, the higher moral standards of humanity.

There was a time when being noble, even if at a personal cost, was the driving force behind people's actions.

Fame, in what now seems like olden times, was not solely reserved for Hollywood celebrities – but also for the likes of Martin Luther King, and Roosevelt, and Gandhi; for writers like Kerouac and Ginsberg and countless others who helped push things forward. JFK was not adored simply because of his charm and good looks, but because his words and actions seemed to represent the best that man could be. When Albert Einstein first visited America, the buzz equaled that of a rock star, and the odd-looking scientist drew crowds of thousands, was on the front page of every paper. These were the types of people once admired and looked up to by our culture.

I cringe when I think about the sorts of famous names our generation will add to the annals of history, and what that will say about us.

"The hottest place in Hell is reserved for those who remain neutral in times of great moral conflict." – Martin Luther King, Jr.

"We have to do the best we can. This is our sacred human responsibility."– Albert Einstein

Words like these once formed part of the greater public discussion, part of the common understanding of who we were. It's as if we still had a link to ancient times. A time when being righteous was cool, and the ultimate personal goal was to do your part to help elevate our society.

The ancient Greeks, fathers of this Western world, often spoke of *arete*. Excellence. A broad and all-encompassing measure of the innate "good" or "quality" of something. From art to philosophy to the daily events in a person's life, *arete* was searched for in everything, especially in oneself. Is this action worthy? Are you fulfilling your purpose to its utmost? Are you living up to your potential? The pursuit of this immeasurable excellence is what motivated people's lives.

This exploration of the best for humankind was the principal aspiration of many of our early cultures. Taoism was the search for the "way" to the fundamental essence of existence. Jews looked to Kabbalah to find a deeper relationship to the universe. Some within Islam studied Sufism. Buddhism and other eastern faiths sought similar sorts of enlightenment. All of these religions and spiritual teachings, from different civilizations in different parts of the world, had the goal of enriching humans' experience on earth. Call it God or Buddha or Tao or qi (chi), the purpose was to evolve, to try and bring humankind higher. This ascent was considered the most important quest we could undertake.

Centuries passed, societies evolved, and the human race progressed. Seeking to break free from the repressive chains of organized religion, modern philosophy and science took over the lead of finding meaning in the world. Scientists and intellectuals and philosophers began to create new theories and schools of thought. But it was really the same old thing – looking for the best way for people to exist in their world. The Age of Enlightenment, Rationalism, Romanticism, Idealism. The greatest thinkers of their time devoting their entire lives to finding new ways and new words to define the higher pursuits of humanity.

Civilization continued to evolve, and the human race finally conquered all of its physical challenges: food, shelter, clothing, nature. Humans became the dominant species on the planet and no longer feared anything. We mastered land, sea, and air. We began to shrink the world into something we could fully examine, fully manage. Science began to explain away our last mysteries, even God. Then came Darwin and the survival of the fittest and the cold realities of one living thing defeating another – and how that was the best way forward. The pursuit of higher understanding left the abstract, came down from the clouds, and got more precise, more individualistic. No longer worried about man's place in the universe, but man's place among man.

The Industrial Revolution came and changed the world forever. Our modern form of capitalism took its hold on civilization. People started talking about social Darwinism and evolutionary ethics. We let transcendentalism and other progressive ways of thinking disappear. Everything became pragmatic and rational. Philosophers and intellectuals got pushed to edges of the public discussion, and industrialists and economists took over the soapbox to declare the best path for human beings to blaze. Laissez-faire capitalism and free markets became the new guiding principles and were praised like the religions of old. We forgot about words like *enlightened* and *righteous*, replaced them with *optimal* and *efficient*. Producing and consuming became the new way forward, material and financial growth the new height of our aspirations.

All the way to today, to where we are now.

Having been raised in this post-postmodern world, completely detached from that ancient way of thinking – a way of thinking sometimes backward and ignorant, but with a pretty clear view of what was really needed and where to look for it.

Without the constant distractions of today's world, our ancestors actually had a minute to sit and think about things. Unburdened by the wealth of crap we have today, people were able to spend some time contemplating what it was they truly needed in their lives.

Humbled by scarcity and harsh realities, raised with the good words of religion, people had a different view of the world and their place in it. They had not yet been convinced of their god-given right to consume their way to personal happiness. They were not yet the centers of the entire universe.

There was a common feeling of responsibility to care about more than your own considerations. An unspoken sense of duty to do something with the blessings you had been given.

People lived their everyday normal lives and did what they had to, but still managed to keep with them certain values. Honor, decency, sacrifice. Concern for the greater good, seeking a righteous way forward, helping thy neighbor.

They were not saints. They didn't have to give it all up or drastically change their lifestyles. It was simply there in the background, in the language, a subtle yet deeply ingrained part of the culture.

Today you can only find that sort of talk in the movies. Those once common words and ways of thinking are so bizarre and foreign to us today that they can only be shown in stories of fantasy, taking place in far-off lands. The noble concepts that average people used to keep close to their hearts can now only exist in movies about sorcerers or world wars, are only believable if spoken by actors with British accents. Otherwise today's crowd just won't buy it, it would be too unrealistic.

Were these good ole ancestors of ours often medieval and barbaric? Did they believe in a lot of ridiculous stuff? Yes, definitely. But that should not take away from the essence of what they understood – and what we can learn from it. Being more advanced does not necessarily mean more evolved.

These people *lived* our past. Their culture was once our culture. If we are now sulking teenagers, they were the innocent children we used to be. Young and immature – but also raw and less jaded and closer to our beginning. Closer to where we came from.

Whether we can see it today or not, there did once exist a different understanding of our place in the world. And if we could pull ourselves away from our own self-centeredness we would see that this old view was in many ways much more enlightened, much more in touch with who we really are and what we really need.

Wandering, questioning, perpetually unsatisfied – human beings have always searched for their place in the grand scheme of things. We have always needed more. By giving a part of themselves to higher pursuits the average person was able to feel as if they were part of something bigger than their own daily lives. And this helped to satisfy some of our innate human dissatisfaction.

It did not need to be said in so many words, it was just how they lived. If we are to be stuck in this tedious everyday life, let's at least aim a bit higher; let's try to live, even in the smallest of ways, the great dreams we have for ourselves.

That's why people followed those righteous old words. That's why they tried to care about something other than their own lives.

Because it made them feel good. Because it worked.

———

I did not start this with a final answer already in hand. I didn't even know the right questions. Not even close.

The only concrete thing in my possession was the unshakeable feeling that things should be different, that there should be more than this. That was the lonely flag I carried and tried to wave high inside myself.

There were inklings of what should be done and where we needed to go, but they were only faint, blurry images. Working my way forward toward these mirages I often became overwhelmed with the task at hand. I felt a burning need to make the solutions real right now, right away. I was so anxious to get somewhere, to finish this thing, that I rushed ahead too quickly.

I was living in the middle of what I was working on, continuously learning and uncovering devastating realities in the world around me, and so faced with these impossible circumstances I could not help but overdo it. Desperately needing there to be a change in the life I found myself living, I imagined the fastest way for it all to happen: global uprisings and progressive paradigm shifts, people suddenly seeing what was wrong and what needed to be done, all of us shaken from our slumber and made to see the light, the brilliant shining light.

But that was too many Hollywood movies. Too many years of epic daydreams. Too many swallowed feelings of disappointment.

I now know that there was never going to be one grand finale, no single happy ending that answered all of our problems. I see that once again the long and sometimes harsh road was necessary. I needed to temper all the pent-up anxiety, all that frustration, and take my time wading through the muddy waters.

So that I could arrive here. Finally able to see that this was always meant to be an evolution, not a revolution.

And evolution is a process that builds upon itself, that takes the best pieces from its past and uses them to go forward.

Everything around us is in some way a product of what came before.

On an island in the Caribbean a species of lizard lives its life, doing its tropical lizard thing. Then one day a dangerous new predator arrives in this lizard's environment and begins killing it off in very large numbers. The males with shorter legs and less speed begin to die off; those with longer legs, and thus able to run faster, survive. Eventually, as time passes and a few generations of breeding take place, this species of lizard develops the permanent trait of longer legs and faster running speeds, allowing it to continue to outrun its opponents and survive in the wild. The lizard we see today did not always exist.

In northern Europe a certain group of bird suddenly shifts its migration patterns, adjusts its nesting spots, and changes its breeding times. This is not done at random. Changes in climate and to their environment cause them to face new conditions – and so they adapt. The shift in migration is to better follow changing weather patterns; the adjustment of nesting spots is to best match new conditions in their environment; and changing their breeding times allows them to be on time for their newborn babies to eat a certain type of worm that now appears a few weeks earlier because of increased temperatures in springtime. At least the birds are doing something about global warming.

Homo sapiens, over tens of thousands of years, developed physical and cultural traits that allowed them to leave their hunchbacked ancestors in the trees and walk upright into today. We have adapted practically every part of who we once were: how our bodies develop, how we ingest food, how we move and how we think – all in accordance to changes in our environment and what was needed to survive. We have changed how we communicate, build our homes, clothe ourselves, and organize our societies – all in an adaption to the new situations we found ourselves in. Everything we now do is built of smaller things we once did.

All of these are different examples of evolution. Do not be scared by the word; *evolution* is simply taking what has worked in the past and using it as part of your repertoire for moving forward. Be it surviving in the tropical jungle, or nesting in the forest, or evolving into the most dominant species on the planet and inventing the Internet.

Evolution is all around us. Happening every day. Right now. As you read this page.

How does a genre of music come to be? Is it spontaneously created out of nothing? Or is it made of the different styles of music that came before it? Taking the best from here and there, absorbing, fermenting, and evolving; evolving into something completely new, but at the same time something built of different pieces from the past.

Our lives are full of things that we think of as fixed, as having always existed in their current form. But most of these are not really fixed at all. Instead they are the result of hundreds or even thousands of years of evolution. Knowledge of the laws of physics, techniques in engineering, the everyday skills of building the foundation of a house or how to best treat a sick patient. These seem to be "facts" taught in our schools, they appear to be "constants" in the living of our daily lives – but they were not immaculately conceived. They originally started out as something different. They were pieced together from what came before them, and then adjusted to fit new conditions, tweaked to fit new information, over and over, tested and revised, shipped across the globe and mixed with something else entirely, until they evolved into what we see today.

The world was once flat, the sun and stars used to spin around the Earth, the church was once the only gateway to salvation. End of story. Written in books and taught to our children as fact.

But none of it was as permanent as we thought. Evolution happened. Things changed. And it will continue to happen. The world will move on, new "facts" will replace old "facts," perpetually until the end of time.

Evolution takes place in the cell and in the microbe, in the smallest of creatures and in the most complex animals. But it also takes place outside of the biological world. Ideas evolve. Languages evolve. Cities evolve. From first sparks of inspiration to fully developed theories; from rough communication to intricate dialects; from one-stop towns to sprawling cities of millions.

From the biological bottom all the way to the most abstract constructions of our civilization, things are constantly evolving.

Physiologically, the human species has already reached a pretty good spot. Our bodies have adapted to the food that we now eat. Our brains have grown large enough to outsmart the bigger animals we share the planet with. Our thumbs are now nice and opposable.

As a society, we have progressed to a point where we have all that we need to survive. We no longer have to live in the forest or roam for a place to settle. We don't have to hunt or gather. We have learned the basics of survival, how to heal the sick and feed our young and work with tools. Our society has learned not only how to survive, but how to flourish. We have expanded across the planet and into the heavens. And we have passed this knowledge on to our young, securing the fate of future generations.

We no longer have to worry too much about those lower levels of our progress. Physically we are already well evolved. And the vital foundations of our society are firmly in place.

At this point in our history the basics are all pretty much taken care of. Evolution has done its job.

So, living in this new position of stability but with things still constantly changing in the world around us, faced with the fact that people today have everything they need to live contentedly yet still feel like something is missing – it is obvious that there's still a need to move forward. We are not yet done evolving.

But how? To where?

What is the next stage in our evolution?

Society: an organized group of people living and working together, with common goals, common interests, etc.

Societies have always been crucial in the development of the individual. Individuals have been forever linked to the group they found themselves a part of, from the school of fish to the tribe living in the jungle. Today we are part of a larger society (modern, capitalist, technological, consumerist, globalized). And for the first time in history the society we live in reaches not only beyond our village and beyond the nearest town, but beyond the borders of all our cities and countries, across oceans and the planet entire. Our society is now *the* society. Of course there are some differences within, but these are becoming increasingly negligible. Language and ethnic differences no longer really separate us. We've got Lonely Planet, and GPS on our phones, and more and more people around the globe now speak at least a bit of English, know what a Big Mac is. For the first time in the history of human civilization more people live in cities than in the countryside. It is now official. Our way of life, our modern society, has taken over the world.

Culture: the shared attitudes, values, beliefs and practices within a group or society.

Art, fashion, media. Common ideas, ways of talking, ways of thinking, morals, and values. "Culture" is the general spirit, the ethos, the zeitgeist of a society.

The culture within a society is a living, dynamic thing. Culture is the personality, the color that fills in the outline. Any group of people can get together and form a society, but it is the culture that develops within that group that truly defines it.

A culture has complex moving parts, parts that are interconnected and that depend on and influence one another. Ideas are expressed through our art; ways of thinking are spread through our conversations and delivered to large numbers by our media; values and morals are passed along to our children who in turn pass them on to their friends. A culture lives and breathes. It consumes what we give it and uses that energy to survive, to grow and change and continue to evolve.

Culture not only gives character to the society, but it also gives it direction. The spirit of a culture will, barring some unforeseen circumstances, decide the fate of the society and the people who live in it.

A culture that promotes war and aggression will forever live with war and aggression. A culture that closes its doors to the outside will never know the beauty lying next door. A culture that cherishes the material will lack the spiritual. One that focuses only on the spiritual will be short on the material.

This is not an ideological rant. Do not be distracted by your political leanings, one way or the other. You can choose any sort of example you want. The point is that our culture influences how we think and act, so it is our culture that will eventually decide if our society lives on successfully or not.

Cultures evolve in similar ways to biological creatures. The evolution of a culture is not that different from the evolution of a species. The thing you see before you – be it a human being or an animal in the forest or the newest trend of a culture – is the end result of countless tiny mutations, an accumulation of what came before.

Everything in our culture, and so everything in our society, is in some way a result of evolution.

The language we speak was once something totally different, the original dialect being one we would not be able to understand today. Over time, as people from different regions mixed, the language changed, adapting to the needs of the people, shedding old expressions that were no longer useful, adding new words and structures that better fit the changing times.

Philosophy, medicine, and physics all push their fields forward by using the knowledge they've inherited and blending it with new discoveries. Fashion and art perpetually take from the past to create their future. Political systems are adjusted and amended to fit new conditions.

Old ways of thinking are constantly being forced to change, from religious and racial prejudice to gender discrimination, evolving over time into new and improved norms for our society.

If something does not evolve, if it does not have what it takes to meet today's new demands – be it an outdated law, ignorant point of view, old way of speaking, or ugly fashion style – the world will move on and it will be left behind.

The success (and the survival) of a culture follows similar rules as those found in nature: take what one already knows and adapt it for new conditions, dropping what is not useful and keeping what works.

A culture, and the society it occupies, must continue to evolve in the right direction or else it will not survive.

But our culture is not evolving properly.

We are not learning from our past.

We are not keeping what has worked and shedding what does not.

We exist solely in this present, unaware of any other past that may have existed, indifferent that an undecided future lies directly ahead.

Nature and culture, mental and physical health, natural resources, and even global climate – all of it mismanaged, abused, brought to the point of destruction. We see that what we are doing is not working, is causing harm, is not up to the standards we should have for ourselves…

But still we continue to bang our heads against the same wall, blissfully ignoring the damage we are causing. We do all the wrong things, harming both our world and our soul, but are too spoiled to see it. Or we see it but are too entrenched, too comfortable, too invested in the illusion, that we will not step away from the enabling teat of this way of life, even for a moment, even as the walls crumble right in front of our eyes.

Are we adapting?

Step back and take a wide-angle view of what we do and how we live. Overwhelming evidence that we must change our polluting ways; yet we resist and fight to keep everything just as it is. Rates of depression and social anxiety through the roof; but we don't change the channel, do not look away from the spectacle, and keep on feeding our young to the beast. Brothers and sisters around the world suffering, literally dying by the millions; and still we allow the corruption, the disgusting greed. Enough food to feed the entire world, enough water for everyone to have a clean cup; but we simply cannot find a way to make it happen, the task supposedly too overwhelming, while trillion-dollar wars are waged and billion-dollar resort hotels are built and the brightest minds of our time hedge their lives away on Wall Street.

Does this sound evolved?

Our world is constantly changing. New conditions and new circumstances are continuously becoming reality. Evolution is happening all around us. Every day. In the physical world and within this human civilization. And so society and its people must evolve right along with it all. It's the only way to stay in rhythm.

If society does not, then evolution and nature will eventually do its job of weeding out the unfit. It may be a slow death: the gradual degradation of morals, economic systems that begin to collapse, civil unrest due to income inequality and poor living conditions. Or it could be a more dramatic decline: severe environmental damage, destructive global wars, depletion of vital natural resources.

In the case of our society any of these is possible.

Whatever the final scenario, not evolving while everything around us does will, at the least, cause us to remain increasingly unfulfilled with our daily lives, increasingly jaded by how badly what we do does not match what we know.

Staying on this same course is not an efficient use of our heritage. We are wasting what we have been given and it is having real-world consequences. Evolutionary theory, natural selection, religious teachings, or just plain old common sense – all would agree that we are not on the right path. That we, in terms of survival of a culture, are very, very far from the fittest.

In ancient times we depended on our culture to help us know how to physically survive day to day. Today, with those daily needs taken care of, we depend on culture to sustain us in other ways. Not to feed our bodies or keep us safe at night, but to satisfy our more abstract needs.

Today we are connected to our culture like never before.

Men do not have to struggle to provide for their families. Women do not have to worry about the well-being of their children. The old social roles are no longer so clear. Sure, the olden days were very tough and personally I'm happy I don't have to work the fields or fetch well water from the next village, but at least those old roles gave people a clear personal purpose, a worthy cause they could devote themselves to and derive satisfaction from.

Today, however, with our society having progressed technologically so far and so fast, there are fewer and fewer places for people to find that sort of simple personal fulfillment.

Evolution has indeed erased most of our old social problems, and that is great, but it has also erased our old social *satisfactions*.

We feel this void – and with the higher purpose of religion and altruism taking a backseat in today's world – we look for that deeper sense of purpose in the society we live in. And this has created a new dependency on today's culture. Without any serious daily challenges for us to tackle and conquer and obtain satisfaction from, we depend on our culture to give some higher meaning to our daily lives. This connects us to our culture in a very profound way.

Unfortunately, the culture we are currently looking to for personal fulfillment is not one that will give us what we truly need. (See: feeding the deepest of our needs the shallowest of things.)

Add to this the fact that our society has explained away all our mysteries, debunked all our myths, put god into a chapter in a textbook, our culture has taken on an even higher level of importance. All of our hopes and fears and abstract human needs now look to this one place. To our culture. And with this culture of ours now dominating everything we see, everything there is to see; with it hitting every blink of our eye, reaching across the globe, into classrooms in Korea and economic decisions in Africa, defining everything we could ever dream of defining, then the health of that culture, the soul of that culture, becomes more crucial than ever.

Because if our culture is everywhere we go and influences everything we have, and if we are connected to this culture like never before, if we derive our very sense of self-worth from it – then if it is sick, if the culture is not evolving in the right direction, it will affect us in the profoundest of ways.

We must realize that we have come too far and are too evolved in every other aspect of our lives and now it's time for our culture to catch up.

The state of our culture is the next battleground. But it's not the sort of cultural argument we are used to having. It's not a decision between liberal and conservative or left and right. History will not give a shit about tax breaks for the rich or how much cheerleading you did for your side. Those are concepts built into the old model, a model obviously outdated. Get your head out of the sand, folks. Stop rearranging the furniture on the *Titanic*.

Our survival as a society, the health of our planet, our happiness as individuals – all depend on moving to the next stage culturally. It's a battle between the pull of true progress and the dragging inertia created by fear and insecurity. And we cannot underestimate its importance.

With our society now dominating the planet, our culture – our attitudes/values/beliefs – becomes the most influential force in the world.

This may sound like a bit of an overstatement, but don't dismiss it just because it sounds big.

The issues that affect us all – political corruption, corporate irresponsibility, economic inequality, destruction of the environment, personal dissatisfaction in our everyday lives – are not caused by problems in the physical world or by a lack of evolution in our base of knowledge. It's not because we are not advanced enough technologically or are missing some material thing.

The issues we face today, every single one of them, are caused by a *lack of evolution in our culture.*

———

Feels like I am getting somewhere. The scattered pieces that had been floating around have now settled a bit more, and have melded into bigger chunks that I can better get a grip on. Things are not coming out exactly as I had planned in that long-ago outline in my mind, but these new pieces seem to fit and lead in the right directions, despite their strange and surprising names.

And it feels right. Not perfect – perfection doesn't exist in this sort of endeavor – but I do feel as though I've finally reduced things down far enough and just might have landed on the right spot. Finally knowing *why* we feel like something is missing. Why among all of this plenty do we need more. Our culture, this culture we have come to depend on so heavily, has not evolved enough. We have surpassed it. We have moved too far ahead. And what we are feeling is the gap between our culture and ourselves.

Yet, like previous revelations, this next step does not allow for much time to celebrate. Because along with some newfound clarity comes the prospect of the next frustration, and in this case, am also being pushed right up against a reality I have always known I would someday have to face. That at some point theory would have to give way to action. That the abstract would eventually have to become at least somewhat practical. That even the most patient of readers would only care for so long about my personal philosophy of everything. That one day I would have to get to work on actually finding a way forward.

No more analysis, no more contemplation. This work was always meant to exist in the real world. I guess I've finally gotten there.

So there is no choice but to look for the next step in our cultural evolution? All right then, let's do it.

Follow the examples of evolution and make sure to learn from what we used to know. Take those old lessons and bring them into today. Keep what was successful and drop what was not.

I reach for what I know has worked in the past and try to cut and paste it into today. I look for the best of what we have done, of what we know, and try to update it, remix it…

But immediately hit a wall.

I know this is where we need to go. Need to rediscover some of those old values and use them to adjust our course. Come on. Look at me. I'm learning more and more every single day, the path getting clearer, the pieces finally coming together.

Yet with every step I take, every thought in the right direction, a door gets slammed in my face. The path both clear and impossible to pass.

Once upon a time I started with faith. With the comforting belief that there is some higher meaning out there for us, that we are not really just running around like ants, floating alone in the dark of space. There is an abundance of historical and clinical research showing how faith can lead to a deep personal happiness – But it doesn't work anymore. Not today. Religion has lost. We can no longer believe its old men. We see the man-made myths and will not ignore our own common sense. It's too late. The curtain has been pulled back.

Moved on to altruism. The selfless giving to others without the thought of recognition or reward. Studies have shown a correlation between charity and feelings of satisfaction and well-being. There are parts of our brain that are positively stimulated when seeing the results of helping others – But don't hold your breath. There will be no great movement of charity and goodwill toward humankind, no matter how much we may need it. We are not there yet. Not there by a long shot. Not with money still dictating everything. And just think about your day. So much to do. We are very, very busy. We'd loved to, if we could just find the time.

Fell back on family. The deepest of our roots. So many of nature's creations feel an innate sense of gratification from reproducing, from seeing their young grow. Raising a family is the most natural of personal satisfactions, from humans to animals and almost everything in between – But we are not penguins. And we are not our grandparents. Things are very different now. Simply raising a healthy family may not be enough to fill the void. We have become very hard to please, and so it's no longer that big a deal. Seeing your kids healthy and fed will not bring you lifelong satisfaction. Not anymore. My grandmother is eighty-eight years old and still only cares if the kids are doing all right, that we are not too skinny; it's literally all she thinks about. But she comes from a very different world than this one. Yes Nona, yes Bubby, we are doing fine. Nothing to worry about here. No Nazis or food shortages or tuberculosis. No worry over a job or school. Everything is just fine. No disaster, no disease, no struggle. No struggle. That mammal-nurturing thing, that deep sense of purpose we used to get from our child-bearing hormones, well, it's been updated for the twenty-first century, and I know that my kid will be able to microwave his or her own frozen meals and that there is a decent office job waiting for them somewhere despite the probable C average. Besides, I see all the overpopulation and overconsumption and hyper-individualism, so propagating my species just doesn't have the same ring it used to.

Scrambled to find freedom. They may take our farms, may take our lives, but they'll never take away our... Yeah, freedom. People living in open democracies report higher rates of "well-being" than those living in repressive nations. Freedom of expression, freedom to choose where you live, whom you marry, vote for, etc., etc. All of these things add to a person's overall happiness. Freedom is super important. I've seen the research. – Alas, this is not Cuba. I was not raised in Saudi Arabia. These freedoms do not increase my current personal happiness because I have lived with them my whole life. They are a given. Of course take them away from me and I will be less happy, but simply having them just as I always have is really just the same old shit for me. Actually, living among all of this "freedom" is a huge part of why I am so fucking depressed with things. Even talking about it pisses me off. Because I see the abuses of this freedom. The waste of this freedom. How the word is used as a cattle prod, a tagline. Words of god from corrupt bishops now replaced by words of freedom from modern-day oligarchal corporatist politicians. Yeah, sure, my freedom to vote for a politician who I know will never do what I really need him or her to. Freedom of the press to feed me generic headlines from the corporate head office. Freedom to be bombarded by a media that is more and more centralized, more and more beholden to advertisers and parent companies. Freedom to protest and take to the streets and make sure the powers that be hear my voice; as long as that voice is not too loud, as long we don't cross this yellow-taped line, as long we don't shake it up too hard or the cameras will be turned off, the swat team lined up. Don't talk to me about freedom. We have no idea what it really is.

So yeah, okay, maybe I need to come down a notch. Out of the abstract and get on the ground. Get my hands dirty with reality.

If we must learn from the past and the past tells us to care for the sake of caring, for no other reason than it being the right thing to do, then I should move onto real-world examples that embody this spirit today.

Activism. Fighting for social justice. Demanding environmental protection.

If the lessons from our more spiritual past tell us that what normal folk need is a sense of greater meaning in their lives, then let's get to it. Let's find out how to integrate those old ways into today's structures.

End poverty. Force corporate responsibility. Raise social awareness.

But again, that wall standing right in my face, towering.

And it is all I can see.

The immense scale of the world's problems and how they grow larger every day. The crucial tipping points and how we are already past them. The corporate callousness, the political donations, the special-interest groups. The greedy creatures literally writing our laws, and running our markets, and steering our ship toward oblivion; while what we are missing, while what I so desperately need, goes not only ignored but openly mocked.

Again I know where we need to go. I can see the path. If we all gave just a bit of our lives to these causes, our combined action could bring about substantial change. We could have the power. The solutions are out there. Waiting for us.

But despite all these years and good intentions and big words and secret preaching, despite finally knowing where we come from and what we really need – I cannot bring myself to do any of it. Not one thing.

Because I know what will happen in the end.

I have seen the future. Seen the good people who actually go out and do what I only talk about. I have walked through the bookstores and seen their spot on the bottom of the shelf. Driven past the rally and seen the sparse turnout. The thousands of well-intentioned magazines, and websites, and small-scale organizations. Devoting their time, trying to get the word out and create positive progress in our world. Taking to the streets and giving up their lives while the rest of us sit at home. I see how they are actually living the theory I have spent so long only thinking about – and I see how, for the most part, it doesn't make much of a difference.

Their passion rising up from the depths of their hearts, coming from a place of pure love and goodwill; but running into not only the tall walls of status quo and human greed, but also the indifference, the apathy, of an entire populace.

Of me.

Now that I know what to take from the past and try to bring to today, now that I've discovered the sort of steps we need to follow – this is what I run into. My own stifling pragmatism. The paralyzing reality that faces all who look up at the mountain. That no matter how right or how wrong, this is a race that simply cannot be won.

So I don't do anything. We don't do anything. And the beat goes on.

This is what happens: Life can be tough. Sometimes downright ugly. Things don't always end up the way we planned. Faced with this difficult reality we unplug and try to find some simple happiness in our everyday lives. But we are smart and educated and so deep down we know that we are unplugging while tough, ugly things are happening, and therefore do not really feel all that happy. Once in a while we break the cycle and get excited and riled up and want to do something different, something other than this. But reality quickly hits us again. And we are overwhelmed and do not know where to start and see that there is probably no point – so we just forget about the whole thing.

Back to the way things were, everything being okay and comfortable, but with looming clouds and lifelong movies and voids you can't stop tonguing.

Over and over until unplugging and digging deeper into your daily life becomes the safest bet, the one thing you can control.

This is where we are.

The shitty reality that things are not as they should be + the even shittier reality that we cannot do anything about it even if we wanted to = discouragement to the point of complete detachment.

We have not only been reduced to apathy, but now begin from this point. Apathy has become our baseline.

But this defeatism – this acceptance without struggle – does not exist as a result of our actually *knowing* that we will win or lose. It comes from how we have been raised, from our modern hardwiring. From the thinking of our dualistic, materialistic culture.

Black/White. Right/Wrong. Big/Small.

You win/I lose.

We are too deep in this culture of immediate success and material goals. Have too long believed that we must be able to touch our achievement, assign it numbers; measure it against something else, from somewhere else; that there is something we must defeat, be bigger than, better than.

So when an average person tries to confront a seemingly massive problem (poverty, pollution, dissatisfaction in his or her personal life) of course the task will feel daunting. And pointless. Without any sign of immediate payoff or quantifiable achievement, we do not see the point in trying. Even if we know that it is the right thing to do – the thing that might finally give us what we truly need – when we stand in front of the gigantic mountain and look at its size, huge and overwhelming, and then look down at the little stones we have to throw and the abstract prizes offered, no kidding we decide to forget the whole idea, no kidding we just go back to what we were doing.

And dig that much deeper.

Something needs to be done, both personally and globally, but people feel that it is an impossible task. We now have a good view of what direction we should be taking, but cannot find a way to take the first step. Cannot find the proper motivation.

So stop. Stop looking at this on the surface. Stop looking at it through the goggles of this result-oriented society. It does not give us the proper perspective.

We must take all these problems and potential solutions and reduce them even further. Break them down some more, down to their lowest level, and see what they are really made of.

Is the problem that somewhere in Africa a little kid is dying of starvation? Or that somewhere in Africa a little kid is dying of starvation *and you know that it could be stopped?*

Are we frustrated because it feels like something is missing from our lives? Or are we frustrated because it feels like something is missing from our lives *and we are giving ourselves to a society that allows this to go on?*

Both, of course. But if the point is to discover how to fit ourselves into this crazy world with a more positive result, then we must always add a deeper perspective to the equation. Our perspective.

It is not simply that there are problems, but that there are problems and we are a part of them. That we wake up every morning and have no choice but to go swimming in the middle of what we know is drowning us.

We are the authors of our own demise. It all comes from us.

Look at the walls and see what they are really made of. Dig at the base of the daunting mountain and see what it actually rests upon. Almost every single thing that might bring dissatisfaction to your life – whatever it may be for you – take that thing that you wish was different and break it apart, piece by piece. Peel the layers off until you get to its core.

And you will find us.

We live and suffer in a world of our own creation. The systems that cause so much harm are built by our hands. The structures that confine us sit on foundations that we have laid.

The corrupt political systems, the greedy corporations, the empty culture, the wasted lives. All of it made of people, by people. Almost any part of our misery can be reduced down to us. Choose something, anything, and if you reduce it down far enough you will find us sitting there, blood on our hands and dumb looks on our faces.

So there is no point in trying to chip away at a problem on its surface. Because the thing you will be attacking does not actually exist: it is really a construction of tiny parts, like a mass of swirling atoms.

Trying to fix something without focusing on what it is really made of is a complete waste of time. It will never work. Trying to reconstruct new models out of the same old parts will only give you new versions of the same problems. And the beat will continue to go on. And we will forever be left dissatisfied with where we are and what is going on around us.

Things will never truly change until we change the roots. Change the building blocks.

Until we change ourselves.

At a young age we began to notice it – a difference between what we felt and how things seemed to be. This happens to every generation; it is a condition of youth.

But this time, and as with no other people in history, the world and all in it could indeed be ours. Nothing was out of reach. In a wave of access to information the likes of which civilization has never seen, nothing was beyond us. Countries, continents, cultures; the ends of our earth, the far-off lands our parents would never see; the sum of all the knowledge our race has ever known – all of it just a flight, a credit card, a click of the mouse away.

From sleeping through science class and the whirling building blocks of life, to surfing through thumbnail pics of the vast expanse of our universe, nobody in the history of our world has ever known as much as we do.

And so we have become hard to please. For good and for bad.

Old, narrow views would no longer be easily accepted. Hypocrisy and supposed morality would be questioned. And eventually, over time, each of us brought our own discoveries into this mix for others to see. And together we have gone forward. Past dirty looks and ignorant prejudices. Past backward thinking and closed eyes. We have embraced strange new neighbors, calling them friend, calling them love. We have broken through the old walls, not because we needed to rebel, but because we learned that it was a better way.

That was the good, living a life those before us could only dream of. But the bad – or maybe not the bad but the inconvenient – is that all this newfound enlightenment lays on us a burden. The burden of knowledge.

Harsh realities will no longer be lost on us. Rights and wrongs will no longer go unnoticed. No matter how hard we may try to ignore them. Despite our best efforts we will see them very clearly and they will stay with us. And mark us. And haunt us.

Until we realize that with all that we have comes a responsibility. Not only to others but also to ourselves.

Because we have come too far.

And we know too much.

To play dumb.

It will no longer work. It simply will not do.

There are no more great mysteries to keep us wide-eyed and occupied. No more ignorance to hide behind. In our rush to progress we have stripped it all away, all of it. And what we are left with today is a complete and unyielding grasp of this world, this life – huge and beautiful and horribly ugly and the only one we have.

Who we are and what we know forces us to look for a better way forward. It is the only way to be truly satisfied. That is our burden.

I come from scorching sun and strange lands, from a young soldier and restless soul. I am the cold forest and innocent love and family lost. I am the humble girl, the three of us left standing, the hand on my face as final caress.

I am the product of everything that ever was! Fortunate sun of the cosmos, swirling gas, molten rock, first spring of life. I am billions of chemical reactions, millions of years of evolution, thousands of ancestors. Generation after generation, coming together, blood and love and struggle and tiny random events – all of it culminating into one single point. Into me.

So do you really think this could ever be enough?

Creatures with hearts and souls expected not to be bothered by the painful inequalities and terrible injustices that surround us. Expected to be satisfied by a culture unworthy of what we are giving it.

All that we have inside. All that ever was. All that will never be.

How can any person of conscience sincerely enjoy their life while people suffer around them, while the world eats itself with greed, and while they give themselves to a culture that allows such shameful wrongs to continue?

The answer is simple. We cannot.

We know that there is so much more that should be happening, we can see it and understand it better than anyone ever has. An entire population with an ancient love burning inside them, fully comprehending the problems facing the world – yet being expected to just forget all that they know, all that they see…and do what? Go back to work? Change the channel? Upgrade their phones?

No way. It won't work. The old tricks will no longer distract us from the inconvenient truths facing our generation. We are too smart for any of that now. Which is why we continue to feel like something is missing even when we have all that we could ever need. Why a society that is at once the most wealthy, most secure, most educated, is also the one with the highest rates of dissatisfaction, social anxiety, and depression. Why a people who literally want for nothing, who have access to almost anything they could ever desire, are also the people with the most obvious cases of restlessness, overcompensation, and addiction.

We may try to ignore these unfortunate facts, may temporarily turn away from the unpleasant sights, but we know what is really going on and we will not feel truly satisfied unless what we do matches what we know. Or at least until we try.

There is a race going on.

It is an eternal contest, going on every minute of every day, from the top all the way down to the bottom. Over time it has taken on many forms. Good versus Evil, Light versus Dark. Ancient mythologies had gods battling each other for dominion over our world. The Almighty and the Devil sat at a chess board and decided the fate of man. A cosmic tug of war between Order and Chaos.

Time passed and new names were given to the conflict. Religion versus Religion. Race versus Race. We believed ourselves advanced and became more intricate in the naming of the opponents: Socialism versus Capitalism. Liberal versus Conservative. Nature versus Industry.

But the names don't matter. It is really just a race against ourselves.

On one side is the relentless advance of the world: Everything that goes on in the world around us. It is a mix of good and bad. The inevitable result of billions of individuals living together, full of their own disparate experiences, desires, and fears. All the ugliness and horrible injustice. All the beauty and tiny acts of kindness. Huge and unstoppable. The world spins on, with or without us, day after day, century after century, and there is nothing we can do about it.

On the other side is our slow progress forward: The snail-like pace of evolution. The gradual opening of eyes and tearing down of walls. It is everything we do to move ourselves forward and keep up with this cold, hard world spinning on all around us.

Take a look at this race from up above. On one side the beat goes on and bad things happen and that is just the way things are and it seems there is nothing we can do about it. On the other side is the slow movement toward something better, the refusal to accept things the way they are, the hope that tomorrow things may be different despite the signs telling us otherwise.

One spirals ahead at high speeds, propelled by our fear and ignorance, swallowing everything in its path. The other crawls forward, fed by education and kindness and enlightenment, trying its best to keep up.

This race goes on every day. All around us our two sides continue to battle one another, and you are a part of it and it affects your daily life whether you decide to care about it or not.

———

We're not far removed from a very barbaric past.

Within our lifetime millions have been murdered because of their race or ethnicity. Innocent people have been persecuted, been made to use different bathrooms and sit in the backs of buses merely because of their color. As recently as the 1990s race was still a major issue. Being an interracial couple was still a big deal, was still considered something scandalous that would elicit looks in the street and drama from the family.

Yet today things seem to have finally changed. A major dividing line drawn between past and present.

Today a mixed-race marriage is not only accepted but is becoming so common we barely notice it. Every second couple I know is mixed in some way or another. Purebred marriages are now becoming the minority. In a few years all our children will be a shade of beige.

A "coloured" man was elected president of the United States of America and my Jewish grandmother has fully embraced my Christian girlfriend. Two events you would have bet strongly against not too long ago.

Racism, although still lingering a bit under the skin, is now the property of the uneducated and the insecure. Nowadays the old arguments and old ways of segregated thinking sound utterly ridiculous. Within a few generations we have turned a thousand years of socially accepted racism into a very serious social taboo; turned it into something to be so embarrassed about you would not even think of expressing it in public. We not only brought this progressive thinking out into the open, but spread it so far across the mainstream culture that it has become the new norm. A new stage in our cultural evolution.

And because our modern society dominates the world, this cultural progression toward an acceptance of people no matter of their background has begun to spread. You see it in our movies and in our television, in the faces that represent us around the globe. And so other countries now see this, absorb it, and with a bit of time and education will begin to make it their own. Just like what happened with the Beatles and blue jeans and hip hop. We set the trend and the rest of the world follows.

Moving past race as a social issue was no small feat, and there was and still is great resistance to it. But it had to happen, evolution called for it. And **we** are the ones that made it happen. Naturally, without even noticing. By doing nothing more than living our lives in a way that felt right – that felt right despite the old social norms telling us otherwise – we put ourselves on the side of progress, of evolution, and pushed the world forward.

Organized religion will be the next to go. One of the last great social barriers and breeding grounds for prejudice, dividing people up based on old fairy tales. It will not last. We will destroy it as well. We will barrel right through this tallest of civilization's walls and we won't even blink an eye.

To an educated person raised in this globalized society, judging a person based on whatever religion he or she happened to be born into will seem absolutely ridiculous. We will not even think of it. Despite generations of our culture telling us otherwise, it will seem medieval and completely absurd. In the not-so-distant future, marriages of mixed religions will seem as normal and accepted as, say, an interracial couple or black man as president.

Give it another generation. A little bit more education and Hollywood movies and Facebook. A few more years of people traveling outside of their borders and meeting new people. Of seeing pictures of their cousins on vacation partying with a pretty blond. Or their friend who just got married to this nice girl whose parents happen to be Lebanese. Just a little more time and you will see this cultural change firmly taking place.

And we are the ones who are making this new future. Simply by going to school, and making friends with new neighbors, and opening our eyes to what needs to happen next. By resisting the backward ways passed down to us and holding onto what we feel is right, we are literally moving our culture up a notch on the evolutionary ladder.

And it has made us happier.

A culture has a soul. It is the collection of our individual spirits, taking the shape of what we feel and how we live. We make the culture what it is.

But at the same time, the spirit of the culture also feeds the individual, completes the definition of who we are. We individuals feed off of the culture and the culture feeds off of us. The individual and the collective constantly define one another.

Therefore if we grew in education and enlightenment, but had to continue to live in a culture that accepted racism and religious intolerance, we would have been severely dissatisfied with our lives, would have been miserable giving ourselves to a society that allowed this to go on.

So we didn't accept it. We felt that it was wrong and did something about it. And changed the world. By moving ourselves forward we moved everything forward. We gave that slow-moving side of the race a little turbo boost and helped push things along.

But it's not enough, we want more.

Turn on the TV and you will see a gay or lesbian character in every other new show. Something absolutely unheard of just a few years ago. And these homosexual characters are no longer typecast as the troubled teen or as flashy, fruity comedy relief; instead they are depicted as everyday people living everyday normal lives, with families and kids and ups and downs just like everyone else. Yes, these families now look different, and the kids may be adopted, and the ups and downs involve new dynamics, but the portrayal is one of everyday normal life. They are normal people, just like you and me.

Our parents resisted this at first, may have dropped some ignorant comments and even put up a big fight – but eventually, and much faster than you would have thought, our elders have accepted this new cultural norm. And they accepted it not only because we pushed it out into the mainstream and in their faces, but because they have been living in this educated period for a while now. So once they got over the initial shock, they too felt that it was right, saw that it was a natural next step for us.

Another wall torn down. Another old skin shed. Another cultural step forward, thank you very much.

The Occupy movement brought hundreds of thousands of people into the streets in cities across the globe. People from all walks of life spending weeks out in the cold for no other reason than a concern for the direction we were headed in. Their persistent protests forced a reluctant mainstream media to cover and discuss the structural problems plaguing our society. They brought the issue of income inequality into the greater conversation and all the way to the presidential election. It may seem that nothing has changed, that the same systematic and moral deficiencies continue, and that the same nearsighted beat goes on. But that's not entirely true. It's not black or white. Despite the apparent return to the same old, something has remained. Something got left behind. As a retreating wave leaves a mark in the sand, we have held onto pieces from those days of enlightenment. They were added to our side of the race, and helped push things in the right direction.

Global warming. Climate change. Fair trade. Hybrid. Eco-friendly. Biodegradable. Sustainable. Renewable. Not too long ago these terms were only in the vocabulary of the scientist or the tree-hugger. Today they are a part of our everyday conversations, have made their way so far across the mainstream that they have very quickly become a part of our everyday lives. In our media, on our store shelves, and in our homes. Even oil-slicked politicians have had no choice but to make these "green" topics part of their repertoire. And again we are the ones who made this happen. Within a few short years we have added a new subject to the greater conversation. By reading and writing and caring, by giving it life with our shopping dollars. Trust me, no company decided to spend money on a new eco-friendly marketing campaign out of the goodness of their heart. Not one single biodegradable window cleaner or all-natural hand soap made it to the store shelf because a corporation decided that changing their existing production line for a more socially conscious one was simply the right thing to do. We made them do it. By caring just a little a bit more about the health of our planet and what we put into our bodies, we forced practically every industry to shift some of their focus toward this greater good. Car companies that once fought to keep us in an oil-burning status quo, now battle one another to come up with the best electric car. Polluting energy companies now spend millions developing alternative energy sources. Every day a new all-natural product appears in our stores. The biggest and most powerful multinational corporation, the mountains that were once too tall, that left us feeling so powerless – now trembling at the sight of us shifting our demands, scrambling to give us what we want.

And again we made ourselves a little bit happier.

———

By knowing the world the way we do, by having this level of power and privilege, we are connected to what happens around us. And because we are this educated, this advanced, we will no longer be as easily satisfied, easily distracted.

It is the price we must pay for all the blessings we have been born into. And we have no choice in the matter. We must pay our toll.

So let's accept our current situation: that we live in a world where we have no choice but to work in tall towers and sit in traffic and toil in the suburbs and bottle our lightning. That is our reality. And it's okay, we gotta do what we gotta do.

But accept this only as a condition we currently live in, not as a definition of who we are. Who we are lies farther ahead.

And it is time to move on.

People derive a personal sense of meaning and value from the society they live in, especially today. And with our old social satisfactions no longer that easy to come by, and with our modern world dominating every aspect of our lives, we look to our culture to help complete the picture of who we are.

So if you are this wonderful, powerful person, a person with love and passion and the whole of history boiling inside you; yet have to be stuck in this modern life, giving yourself up to its daily comings and goings, swallowing the big dreams you once had, then you need to see that it is worth it, that this something you are a part of has true value, that it is worthy of what you are giving to it.

And if it does not, if the world we live in does not yet match the high standards we need for ourselves, then we must not go gentle into that good night. If what we have been doing is not working, if this modern experiment – with all its wonderful achievement and amazing distraction and unimaginable excess – still leaves us feeling like something is missing…

Then we must look elsewhere.

Let's take that lesson from our past and use it to move ourselves forward. Let's be truly evolved. Let's drop what is not working. Let's hold on to what we really need: To struggle. To reach higher. To discover and achieve and explore. Read our ancient stories, think of the movies we love, the songs that move us. All of them speak in some way to that indefinable human need for something more.

We have to take the next step. We are done here.

Let's face the irreconcilable truths of our generation and try our best to reconcile them: that we are big and beautiful and need more / that this is not enough for us.

But do not run from the conflict. Take it in. And be happy that it hurts. The pain, the dissatisfaction in your daily life, means that we are ready to move forward. Means that we are done with all of this.

Accept the two opposing realities and relish their bittersweet conflict: that we love this world and long to be happy within it / that we hate this world and want a better one.

It is in this conflict that lies the key.

There is nowhere else to go. Nothing left to do. So it is here that I need to learn to live, in this beautiful, terrifying nowhere land.

It is the only place big enough.

Yes I am a nameless number. Yes I am a tiny piece lost in a giant puzzle. But still, I will do what I can. Even if it's in the dark. Even if I'm tucked far away in the back and nobody can hear me but me. Even if, in the end, it doesn't make much of a difference.

I will change the channel until I see something of true value. I will ignore your advertisements until they show some conscience. I will boycott your product until you demonstrate social responsibility.

If your song is manufactured fluff, I will not buy it. If your movie is cheap and thoughtless, I will not watch it. If you speak with money or greed as a motivation, I will ridicule you. If your actions or inactions lead to pain or suffering, I will fight you until you are no more.

I will demand the truth, ignore the bullshit, and watch the world change.

We are already doing it. Even if it's sometimes hard to see. Evolution is happening within me, and therefore is happening to our culture, and in turn to everything that we know. The world is being pushed forward with every word I write, every word you read. With every friend you make, every wall you refuse to see, every old way you help turn into ancient history.

This is the only thing left for me to do and so I will do it.

Because it will make the world a better place.

Because it will make me happier.

Because they are one and the same.

I've tried my best to be honest here. To remember and recount what it was that I felt and thought, hoping that the stops along my way were similar to yours, hoping that by more clearly seeing the paths behind us we might be better able to shed some light on the ones lying up ahead.

It has not been easy. Sifting through a lifetime of random scribblings, categorizing your life's experiences into what may or may not be useful, micromanaging your most personal thoughts and trying to sum it all up into something coherent, something that must make sense in the real world. It's pretty humbling. You see a lot of where you went wrong, of how big a part you've played in your own story.

The sense of urgency definitely remains. I still worry that my time is running out, that I am one step away from giving up, accepting that this is it. But I no longer have an uncontrollable urge to run off and search somewhere else. Because I am here, working on this. Completely opened up, insides raw from all the rummaging around and inspection. But still here.

History neatly packages up the past for our viewing pleasure, with names and summaries we can easily judge as good or bad, success or failure. Unfortunately those living in the present never have the benefit of such hindsight, never see a dime of their prize money. It always gets paid out in the future.

Do I wish there were a simpler ending to this? One big conclusion that wrapped things up neatly and allowed us all to finally breathe that sigh of relief? Of course. But that's not how this sort of story goes.

Tomorrow will come and it will be very similar to today. All around me there will be signs of impending doom and slim glimmers of hope.

So all we have is today. Plain old today. No page in a history book, no epic movie. No revolution, no grand climax, no final accomplishment that you can name or frame or email to your friends.

But still it can be glorious.

As simple a thing as teaching your child to be open-minded, to embrace what moves us forward and reject what holds us back. As seemingly inconsequential an act as shopping with a conscience, of buying products that help rather than harm.

The world is big and cold and spins on without a care – but it is also tiny and interconnected and dependent on us. So don't give yourself away too easily. Demand a bit more. It will do a lot more good than you realize.

This can be our small part to play in the never-ending battle. Our way to leave our mark, be immortal, fill a bit of the infinite void. Finding some deeper satisfaction not in one big fancy event, but as an everyday part of who we are. The revolution happening as evolution.

For now I'm going to close up the computer and pack it in for the day. Gotta go. Time for dinner, have to take out the garbage, pick up the kids, get ready for work...

But it's okay.

I'll be back tomorrow.

———

Special thanks to all of those who cared enough to love and bleed and let it all hang out. Your brave words and beautiful music let me know that I was not alone. Without you I never would have had the guts to do this.

Jason Najum
November, 2012
Montreal, Canada

Please support the book by sharing with your friends and posting a review

Visit the author's website and read his blog at
www.jasonnajum.com

Endnotes

1. "Stand arms outstretched. Stare the sun down. Swallow poison. Scream my lungs out until it fills this room." Adapted from the song "Indifference", lyrics by Eddie Vedder, performed by Pearl Jam, Epic Records, 1993

2. "Trading magic for fact, no trade backs." Adapted from the song "I'm Open", lyrics by Eddie Vedder and Jack Irons, performed by Pearl Jam, Epic Records, 1996

3. "Is this a test...it has to be." Adapted from the song "The Patient", lyrics by Maynard James Keenan, performed by Tool, Volcano Entertainment, 2001

www.ingramcontent.com/pod-product-compliance
Lightning Source LLC
Chambersburg PA
CBHW022112280326
41933CB00007B/348